THE FOOD OF
SINGAPORE

Authentic Recipes from the Manhattan of the East

Recipes by Djoko Wibisono and David Wong

Photography by Luca Invernizzi Tettoni

Introduction by Lee Geok Boi

Edited by Wendy Hutton

Produced in association with The Beaufort Sentosa

PERIPLUS
EDITIONS

Published by Periplus Editions (HK) Ltd.

Copyright © 1994 Periplus Editions (HK) Ltd.
ALL RIGHTS RESERVED
Printed in the Republic of Singapore
ISBN: 962-593-007-8
Address all inquiries and comments to:
  Periplus (Singapore) Pte. Ltd.
  Farrer Road P.O. Box 115, Singapore 9128

Publisher: Eric Oey
Design: Peter Ivey
Art Direction: Luca Invernizzi Tettoni &
  Christina Ong
Cover Illustration: Daniel Wegera
Managing Editor: Mike Cooper
Production: Mary Chia & Teresa Tan
Marketing Director: Julian Sale

Distributors
Singapore and Malaysia:
  Berkeley Books Pte. Ltd.
  Farrer Road P.O. Box 115, Singapore 9128
Indonesia:
  C.V. Java Books, Box 55, JKCP, Jakarta 10510
Thailand:
  Asia Books Co. Ltd.
  5 Sukhumvit Soi 61, Sukhumvit Road, P.O. Box 40
  Bangkok 10110
Australia:
  Viking/ Penguin Books Australia Ltd.
  487 Maroondah Highway, P.O. Box 257
  Ringwood, Victoria 3134

Acknowledgements
The publishers and The Beaufort Sentosa would like to thank the following for their generous assistance in providing tableware, furniture and other decorative items for use in this book: Abraxas; Blue Moon; Tang's Studio and The Atelier.

Thanks also to the following restaurants for their kind cooperation in arranging location photography: Hua Yu Wee Seafood Restaurant, Komala Vilas, Muthu's Curry Restaurant, Alkaff Mansion, Aziza's Restaurant, Tai Thong Restaurant and Li Bai Restaurant.

A BEAUFORT HOTEL
SENTOSA, SINGAPORE

ABRAXAS

BLUE MOON

TANGS STUDIO

Contents

Part One: Food in Singapore

A tropical metropolis with a voracious appetite

Situated at the tip of the Asian mainland, Singapore is a tiny island nation that appears as a speck on the world map. Beginning as an insignificant fishing settlement a little over one and a half centuries ago, it grew to an important British colonial entrepôt. Since becoming an independent republic in 1965, Singapore has developed into one of Asia's most dynamic and modern cities with a GNP that is the size of many larger nations.

Skyscrapers, highways and air-conditioned shopping centres crammed with luxurious status symbols from around the world replace the more traditional Asian vistas of paddy fields and palm-fringed beaches. Singapore's highly regulated system of government has produced the ultimate consumer society which might, at first, seem lacking in passion and individuality. But when it comes to the subject of food, Singaporeans reveal their true identity. Food is, quite simply, the national obsession.

This is a country where food goes with everything and no decent meal is complete without an extended discussion about the food being enjoyed or the next meal. Eating out is a family activity and, for many, a daily routine. This habit has virtually created a national identity defined by the cuisine: not just any food but the multi-ethnic fare served in unpretentious restaurants and food centres throughout Singapore. This food is prepared by cooks who once plied the streets or set up temporary stalls along the back lanes of the city. Although these cooks have now been given permanent locations in food centres or upmarket air-conditioned food courts, Singaporeans still refer to their cuisine as hawker fare.

Few Singaporeans give much thought to the origins of what they are enjoying in this multi-racial society—what matters is the taste. Typical Singapore food is actually a blending of the cuisines of the different peoples who have settled here. Dinner could be Chinese-style soup and vegetables and a Malay chicken curry. Breakfast could be cereals and milk or Indian *dosai* with *dhal*. Even eating styles are a blend. One person sitting at the same table may eat his plate of rice with fork and spoon, while another eats with chopsticks, and a third uses his fingers.

The Singapore food scene is full of powerful aromas: garlic and lard sauteed in a hot pan, sticks of satay grilling over an open flame, dried shrimp paste roasted before grinding, sizzling ghee on a hot griddle. These are some of the smells that trigger memories of home for Singaporeans, descendants of migrants who brought with them rich food traditions from all over Asia. There is in Singaporeans the spirit of adventure when it comes to food: "It's new, it's different, so we must try it out."

Opposite:
The skyline of Singapore, seen from the south, reveals a thoroughly modern city under a tropical sunset.

Money Can Buy You Everything

*A garden city where food
is imported from around the world*

Thanks to its location just over 1 degree or about 137 kilometres north of the equator, Singapore's climate is humid and steamy all year round. Tropical rains frequently bring freshness to the afternoons, and in contrast with the usually hot days, nights are balmy and the early mornings cool.

Dense equatorial rain forests and the few low hills which once shaped the landscape have long given way to an equally dense cover of high-rise office blocks, shopping complexes, condominiums and public housing. Now the tropical humidity and heat are kept at bay by air-conditioning, and the steel

Singapore offers consumers just about anything they want from around the world, especially when it comes to food.

and concrete high-rise jungle is softened by the numerous trees and little parks which have earned Singapore the label "Garden City". Busy highways are divided by tall trees and flowering shrubs.

Amidst all this green and blooming lushness, you would be hard put to find a farm, unless it's the indoors hydroponic variety. Singapore has grown almost none of its food for decades, preferring to devote scarce land to industry and housing for its population of just over three million.

However, money can buy you everything and sitting at the hub of a region which is still largely agricultural, Singapore imports its food and even water from its neighbours to the north and south. Since Southeast Asian markets do not carry all the produce and fine foods to which affluent, globe-trotting Singaporeans have become accustomed, its excellent air and sea connections bring in the best from all over the world.

With produce coming in from all over, the island also marks the passage of the seasons around the world. The Thai and Indian mango season in April and May finds fruit shops here awash in scrumptious and cheap mangoes. It's summer and cherries abound in California? They do too in Singapore. Is it the season of the hunt already? Then premier restaurants around town will soon have game on the menu. And everyone knows when durians are in season. The pungent smell, fragrant or awful depending on your affection for this thorny fruit, makes it hard to ignore.

Garbage collectors certainly cannot ignore the literally tonnes of thorny shells.

If seasonal foods mark the passage of spring, summer, autumn and winter in different parts of the world, then paradoxically few foods are out of season since Singapore buys from countries both north and south of the equator, catching the seasonal produce from all over.

Constant saturation does lead to a jaded palate and food importers have to work hard looking for new and novel produce to tempt bored Singaporeans. The list of countries which supply Singapore with produce or food products is growing constantly as buyers wander further afield. However, not everything consumed in Singapore is imported. The country does have a very tiny group of farmers, some of whom grow mainly leafy vegetables and fruits while a few high-tech farmers do their farming in multi-storey factories, growing vegetables without soil in trays of nutrient-rich water and mushrooms in sawdust.

There is also farming of both marine and freshwater fish and prawns. Fish farmers have to work hard to keep up with the voracious demand for live seafood in restaurants. Being an island once inhabited by fishermen, it is no surprise that in Singapore, seafood is a popular item in everyone's diet.

Seafood also avoids various religious strictures: Muslims do not eat pork; Hindus and strict Buddhists avoid beef and many Chinese find lamb and mutton a trifle strong.

No matter how high-tech, local fish farming and the few local fishermen cannot keep up with demand and the island imports most of its fresh seafood. While much comes from the fishermen of the region whose fishing boats unload their chilled catches in Singapore, the more expensive seafood such as *sashimi*-quality fish comes in by air.

The abundance of quality produce gives creative cooks plenty to work on. The multi-ethnic population, well-travelled and well-heeled, are not only sources of culinary inspiration but also avid supporters of the country's food industry.

Creative restaurant chefs on the look-out for something new to excite the palates of Singaporeans are increasingly experimenting with new ingredients and new styles. Starting with a culinary heritage based on some of Asia's greatest cuisines—Chinese, Indian, Malay and Indonesian—they borrow from other Asian neighbours, experiment with western ingredients and styles, mix something from here with something from there. Like everything else in Singapore, food is definitely on the move.

Singapore Style

Where a variety of cuisines have met and mingled and the search for culinary excitement continues

Right:
The recently restored Clarke Quay area along Singapore River is an ideal setting for alfresco meals.
Opposite:
A bygone age of elegant dining is recaptured at the hilltop Alkaff Mansion.

When Stamford Raffles, the British founder of modern Singapore, declared the little fishing village and occasional pirates' den a free port in 1819, he drew in swarms of migrants in search of economic opportunities. The Chinese, especially from the southern coastal provinces of Fujian and Swatow, came by the shipload, fleeing the chaos of a dynastic changeover. The northerners were very much in the minority, as was the case with the Indian community which began with a small contingent of Indian soldiers in the British army. Not long after being declared a free port, Singapore was designated an Indian penal station and convicts were sent here to work on public buildings. British labour policy also brought in droves of Tamils from south India as indentured labour for public works.

The island's small Malay population swelled with newly arrived Javanese, Sumatrans, Boyanese from Madura and other Indonesian islanders, as well as both Malays and Straits Chinese from Malaya. Arabs and Jews came from the Middle East; there was a fairly large community of Armenians and, of course, a strong enclave of Britons who administered the colony. By the end of the 19th century, Singapore was perhaps the most cosmopolitan city in Asia. The migrants had come from places with long established culinary traditions. Now began the process of blending which has produced some of Singapore's most interesting dishes, even cuisines.

The hybridisation began the day a Malay girl married a Chinese man to form the first of the Straits or Peranakan Chinese. Not all *babas* (Peranakan men) and *nonyas* (Peranakan women) had a Malay ancestor, but they were distinguished from the more recently arrived Chinese by the Malay dress of the womenfolk and by their cuisine. Straits Chinese or *nonya* cusine combined the Chinese affection for pork prohibited to Muslim Malays with Malay ingredients such as coconut milk, fragrant roots and herbs, chillies and dried spices for character. Certain Chinese dishes such as braised pork were not ignored, but took on a Singapore overtone with the

Some ancient Chinese traditions live on in modern Singapore, where a teahouse offers a chance for repose while drinking a specially brewed pot of tea.

Belacan or chilli sauce. Neither does the community forget its Indian roots in certain dishes such as Vindaloo, a pork curry tarted up with vinegar, and Devil Curry which, as its name implies, can set your tongue on fire.

Even without intermarriage, it is not possible to live cheek by jowl with someone of another ethnic community without picking up ideas on food. Perhaps surprisingly, the British, not noted for their cuisine, were also sources of inspiration. The colonial *memsahibs* employed Hainanese boys as cooks and they interpreted western cuisine for the colonial masters in a way which produced Singaporean classics such as Hainanese pork chops: breaded pork fried in oil, then dressed with potato, tomato wedges, green peas and onion in a gravy of soy sauce thickened with starch.

Cuisines with more flourish than British have also taken on Chinese airs in Singapore. When a Singaporean thinks of Indian food, he thinks of fish-head curry, which is a dish that no son of India has heard of until he comes to Singapore. The Indians may eat curry but only the Chinese have the tradition of eating such things as heads, tails, ears and entrails. Mee Goreng, again sold only by Indians, is another Singapore Indian classic not found in India since yellow Hokkien noodles (*mee*) cannot be found there.

While Straits Chinese cuisine may be Chinese food with strong Malay overtones, Malay food has also incorporated Chinese ingredients such as noodles, beansprouts, beancurd and soy sauce. This has produced Singaporean Malay dishes such as Mee Soto and Tauhu Goreng.

addition of lemon grass and galangal, and many a bland Chinese dish was given a shot with pungent Sambal Belacan, a spicy condiment of dried shrimp paste and chillies.

Another community, the Eurasians, also developed a hybrid cuisine which shares much with Straits Chinese cuisine but does not forget its European roots in its focus on roasts, steaks and chops seasoned with soy sauce and eaten with Sambal

Chinese food itself has evolved with distinctive Singapore touches which show the influence of the other ethnic communities. Hainanese chicken rice may sound like it comes from the Chinese island of Hainan. It was once prepared only by the Hainanese in Singapore but you would be hard put to find it on Hainan, especially that critical accompaniment of chilli sauce made of fresh ginger, chilli and vinegar.

While chillies may not be native to Southeast Asia, it is hard to imagine any Chinese noodle or rice dish without chillies. Every home and most restaurants stock chillies in one form or another, regardless of race or culinary preferences.

Singapore's prosperity is taken for granted by the huge middle class. With the wherewithal to travel beyond the confines of a very small country, to eat and drink well, they carry on the tradition of eating out which started when the menfolk did not have the time to do their own cooking and thus depended on itinerant hawkers.

This practice is now fuelled by the growing number of women working outside the home. Eating out and constant exposure to good food have encouraged hybridisation of the cuisine and a highly competitive food business has to keep tempting Singa-

poreans with new dishes to stay in business.

The range of what people eat has grown tremendously. A proper meal once consisted only of rice and some dishes. Today sandwiches, burgers and pizzas go down just as well as noodles and rice. Singaporeans eat very eclectic meals with components or dishes from different cuisines, and even eating styles are as eclectic.

Different communities eating together means the host has to be mindful of religious strictures and choose food acceptable to all. Hindus will not eat beef, Muslims will not eat pork, and some Chinese do not enjoy mutton or beef. Malay and Indian food pose no problems, and Chinese food being highly adaptable can now be found in *halal* Chinese restaurants conforming to Muslim dietary restrictions; these even attract Chinese customers who can now eat comfortably with their Muslim friends.

Adaptability and spotting an economic opportunity have been watch-words with the migrant communities from the beginning. Culinary purity loses out to a general devotion to seeking the flavourful. The resulting mix has made the Singapore food scene more lively and far richer, introducing unique combinations which did not exist in the culinary traditions from which they stem.

Festivals, such as the Muslim Hari Raya at the end of the fasting month of Ramadan, provide an opportunity for feasting as well as for family reunions. Visitors of all races are welcome during the traditional "open house".

Chinese Food

Hokkien, Teochew and Cantonese cuisines from southern China predominate

W‌hen two Chinese meet, the traditional greeting is to ask whether the other has eaten, highlighting the central place of food in Chinese civilisation. The greeting must surely have been brought about by the cycles of famine long a part of Chinese history, which have made Chinese cooks firm followers of the adage "waste not, want not." This approach to food is also characteristic of a people with strong roots in the soil; you ate whatever was plentiful, or in season, and you made the best you could of it. And Chinese everywhere, including in Singapore, do make the best of everything they can get their hands on.

A little can go a long way when there are several kinds of ingredients cut small, tossed into a hot *kuali* (wok) with a little oil and stir-fried with fragrant garlic and salted soya beans. Cutting food into bite-size pieces makes for rapid, even cooking. Small pieces are also easier to eat when you are manipulating two thin pieces of wood to pick up your food, and they simplify sharing in the communal style of eating. Although large chunks of meat are not unknown, these are braised until the meat falls away from the bone and can be eaten in bite-sizes, or else the meat is cut into small pieces before being taken to the table.

While stir-frying is very Chinese, so is steaming where the prepared food is placed in bamboo steamers over a *kuali* of boiling water. Equally popular is braising or stewing, long slow cooking with such basic seasonings as garlic, soy sauce, bean paste or oyster sauce which turns tough cuts into flavourful melting morsels. Deep-frying or stir-frying are sometimes combined with braising or steaming. A sauce can be prepared with stock, rice wine, soy sauces, sweet-smelling greens such as spring onions and coriander leaves and other colourful vegetables, to be poured over the deep-fried ingredient.

Many Chinese dishes combine several vegetables with meat or seafood, making for naturally colourful food. Pit-roasting is another cooking technique to get that delicacy of roasted suckling pig, and var-

Opposite:
Elegant Chinese restaurants such as Li Bai serve impeccable Cantonese cuisine to discerning gourmets.
Left:
The nucleus of Chinatown is now encircled by modern skyscrapers.

ious roasted meats are done in kiln-like ovens or large drums although Chinese "roast" chicken is actually deep-fried.

Although the basic cooking techniques are used by Chinese everywhere, different provinces tend to prefer certain techniques and prefer different ingredients. Northern cuisine has mutton dishes, unheard of in the south, which accounts for the unfamiliarity of the Chinese in Singapore with mutton. Northern cooks are also more heavy-handed with garlic and bean paste, while cooks in Sichuan and Hunan on the northwest rely on chillies as well. Northerners eat *mantou*, a wheat-flour bread as a staple, although rice is more usual in the south.

The food of all regions of China is represented in Singapore. There is both elegant Shanghainese and Beijing cooking, the stuff of imperial kitchens, as well as spicy Sichuan and Hunanese food. From the south comes Cantonese cuisine which can range from elegant *nouvelle* Hongkong with its small portions and fruity flavours, to hearty, homely Sa Poh (braised) food cooked in claypots. Cantonese roast meats such as suckling pig, roast pork and red-roasted pork (Char Siew) are justifiably popular. Cantonese Dim Sum or "little hearts" go down well the world over and Singapore is no different. Dim Sum is especially popular for lunch, whether quick or leisurely. In Singapore, the Hokkiens (originally from Fujian province) are the largest dialect group, followed by the Teochews (from Swatow), then the Cantonese. The relatively small size of the Cantonese community is not obvious given the high profile of Cantonese cuisine in Singapore. By contrast, fewer restaurants serve the more homely Hokkien food with its characteristically hearty braised dishes such as Tau Yew Bak (pork braised in black soya sauce) eaten with steamed buns, oyster omelette and Popiah (spring rolls in soft wheat skins).

The cuisine is strong on pork dishes, especially "white pork" meat with plenty of marbling, trotters complete with the fatty skin, or belly pork. Garlic and soy sauce are used generously. Soups are good, especially heavy soups with meatballs and vegetables.

One Hokkien contribution to Singapore hawker food is Hokkien *mee*, the yellow wheat noodles found not only in Hokkien Fried Mee or Hokkien Prawn Mee, but also in Malay Mee Rebus or Soto Mee, and Indian Mee Goreng. In fact, much of the character of the food cooked by once-mobile hawkers now located in food centres comes from the wide range of ingredients used by different dialect

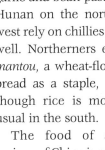

Cantonese cuisine is a perennial favourite, especially the tidbits known as dim sum, enjoyed here in a typical Chinatown tea-house cum restaurant.

groups, put together in different ways by other communities.

Teochew food is characterized by steaming, light soups and fish dishes because many in the community were, and still are, in the seafood business. Like yellow Hokkien *mee,* the Teochew fishball is a classic ingredient accepted by all races and found in many dishes be it Indian Rojak, Malay *sambal* or Chinese noodle soup.

The fishball is made by pounding fish meat with salt and water to get a bouncy fish paste. The same fish paste can be used to make fishcake, again another essential garnish in Singapore food. Equally light and very popular not only for breakfast but lunch, dinner and supper is Teochew savoury porridge, rice gruel eaten with various boiled, stewed, steamed and fried dishes, whether cooked at home or eaten at porridge restaurants.

Hua Yu Wee Seafood Restaurant is one of the last of the old-style Bedok restarants, where sumptuous seafood is enjoyed in the garden of a bungalow set along Singapore's east coast.

Although it may appear that the Chinese live only to eat, they also eat with health in mind. Long before the link between food and health became fashionable, the Chinese were developing a complex philosophy on dietetics. Certain foods were "cooling" or *yin,* others "heaty"or *yang* and some were neutral. The human constitution was classified the same way, with some people being more *yin,* others more *yang.*

Balancing the *yin* and *yang* in your body by eating the correct foods kept you in good health, and it was therefore important to eat anything in moderation and to eat a wide range to get the right balance. The concept is thought-provoking and certainly it remains a great conversation topic for Singaporeans of all races at meal times.

Malay Food

The fragrant link
between Thailand and Indonesia

Fragrant rhizomes such as galangal (*lengkuas*), ginger and fresh turmeric, together with shallots, garlic, fresh and dried chillies, with emphatic overtones from lemon grass (*serai*) and dried shrimp paste (*belacan*) are what make Malay curries different from Indian ones. Malay cuisine is the link between Indonesia, to the west and south, and Thailand to the north. Although the results are rather different, there is a certain amount of overlap, especially with the food of nearby Sumatra and, in the northern states of Malaysia, with Thailand.

The rhizomes and seasonings typical of Malay food can also be combined with spices like coriander, cumin and fennel, although not as commonly as in Indian curries. Coconut milk, widely used in Southeast Asia, is used liberally to enrich many Malay dishes. Malay food also tends to be slightly sweet with the addition of palm sugar or white sugar, while juice from the sour fruity tamarind adds tang and subtlety.

Although Malay food is not as prominent in Singapore as Chinese, it is nonetheless part of the mainstream diet. Familiar favourites are the Malay classics like Korma, Rendang, Chicken Curry and the various *sambals*. Sambal Belacan is so accepted that it even appears as a standard condiment in Teochew restaurants, complete with half a lime.

Nasi Lemak, a coconut-rich rice dish served with a variety of accompaniments such as crisp fried anchovies (*ikan bilis*), peanuts, prawns, shredded omelette and chilli *sambal* is what many Singaporeans eat for breakfast. Some of the *kuih* (cakes) associated with the *nonyas* were Malay to start with, and along with Chinese Chui Kuih (steamed rice cake with preserved vegetables) and Indian Roti Prata are consumed for breakfast and at tea-time.

In Singapore the highlight of Malay cuisine is satay, thought by some to have derived from the Arab *kebab* but with a character all its own. Satay has even spawned two Chinese versions: Satay Chelop and Nonya Pork Satay, as well as the hawker dish of Satay Bee Hoon.

On the other hand, Roti John ("John's bread") was said to have been inspired by a homesick tourist named John who, so the story goes, was in search of a sandwich. A helpful hawker sliced up a loaf of French bread, clapped in a mixture of minced mutton and onion and dipped the whole in beaten egg which he fried until crisp. If the tourist named John was bemused, locals took to Roti John and it is now a staple at Muslim food stalls. It is more likely, however, that Roti John is an adaptation of Murtabak, an Indian Muslim dish which is the Asian answer to the Italian pizza.

Opposite: Undoubtedly Singapore's best known Malay restaurant, Aziza's, located in historic Emerald Hill, takes its name from its charming owner.

Indian Food

Curry and company
plus dishes unknown in the sub-continent

The Indians, who form just over seven percent of Singapore's population, are predominantly from the south of the sub-continent: mostly Tamils from Tamil Nadu, as well as numbers of Malayalees from Kerala, in the south west. Like the Chinese, the southerners arrived first and came in larger numbers compared to northerners such as the Sindhis, Gujeratis, Bengalis and Punjabis. Naturally, southern Indian cuisine is more established and more common than that of the north.

Indian vegetarian restaurants offer magnificent vegetable creations as well as fabulous breads and (seen in the glass display cases) rich milk-based cakes and sweetmeats.

Even non-Indians can easily tell the more fiery southern food from the milder northern dishes. Indian cooking calls for spices such coriander, cardamom, cumin, fennel and cloves, but north and south use them differently. North Indian food is enriched with yoghurt or cream, with a blend of chopped herbs, fresh chillies, and tomatoes added late in the cooking for a subtle flavour. These thicker curries are eaten with a variety of breads from unleavened flat *chapati* to puffy *tandoor*-baked *naan*. Singapore's North Indians, like North Indians elsewhere, have a largely wheat-based diet, although they eat at least one meal of rice daily.

South Indians, on the other hand, eat a rice-based diet which suits their more liquid curries which are often enriched with coconut milk. However, the southerners have their breads too: fluffy and ghee-rich *roti prata*, often the choice for a full breakfast, and *dosai*, tangy pancakes made from a fermented rice and *dhal* batter. *Dosai* do nicely for breakfast, lunch, tea and dinner, especially when they come in a variety of forms from crisp and paper-thin to fat and fluffy, plain or with curry filling. *Dosai* shops are also often vegetarian restaurants since vegetarianism is mandated by Hinduism.

Named after the "plate" on which the food is served, these "banana leaf restaurants" solve the problem of washing up by having customers eat off banana leaves. Rice is surrounded by your choice of several types of vegetable and *dhal* curries, crisp *pappadam,* cooling yoghurt and tangy *resam* (pepper water).

Some banana leaf restaurants cater to carnivores, offering meat and seafood curries, the most popular being fish-head curry, a dish that most think of as Indian but is in fact Singapore Indian.

While Singapore Indian food has most of the characteristics of Indian food elsewhere, it has not escaped the influences of other ethnic communities. Apart from fish-head curry, another local Indian favourite is Indian Mee Goreng, fried wheat noodles prepared with chillies, potato, beansprouts and some curry gravy.

There is also Indian Rojak, which has some rather un-Indian ingredients such as Javanese *tempeh goreng*, Chinese fried *tauhu* and fishcake among the boiled potatoes, hard-boiled eggs in batter and a choice of fritters, all eaten dipped in either a sweet, starchy sauce or chilli sauce.

Mutton soup is another dish with a Chinese accent: lots of fresh coriander to perk up the robust soup seasoned with spices. The soup comes invariably with crusty *roti perancis* (French bread). South Indian food is often prepared by Indian Muslims, some of whose restaurants along North Bridge Road are well-known for their Murtabak (stuffed fried pancake) and Biryani, a fragrant saffron-coloured rice flavoured with fried onions, spices, raisins and nuts, cooked with mutton or chicken.

A feature of Indian food is the extensive use of dried beans and lentils in a variety of ways from staples to snacks. This gives Indian food a clout with vegetarians of all races.

One meat eschewed by both North and South Indian cooks is beef, because of religious strictures imposed by Hinduism which venerates the cow.

So-called "banana leaf restaurants" offer a selection of food served on the original disposable plate. Here, offerings include the famous Singapore Indian dish, Fish-head Curry, as well as succulent crabs and spicy prawns.

Another is pork, this time because it is prohibited to Muslims. The Mughal Emperors and their court were Muslims, and it has become traditional in India and Indian restaurants the world over not to serve either pork or beef. Indian food is therefore always *halal* (conforming to Muslim dietary laws). This makes it a favourite for multi-racial gatherings in Singapore, giving Indian food an impact out of proportion to the small size of the community.

ROTI
MURT

INDIAN ROJAK
RE-FRIED HOT&CRISPY

ROTI JOHN~MURTABAK THOSAY
MUTTON CHICKEN MUTTON CHICKEN
$3.00 $4.00 SMALL$3.00 SMALL$4.00
MED$5.00 MED$6.00

MIX
VEGETAB

SOYA BE
PEANUT

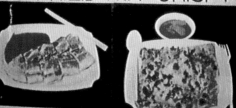

JOHN BAK (THOSAY)

ITEMS	PRICE
CUTTLEFISH	BETWEEN SIZE
FRIED EGGS	$0.50
PLAIN FLOUR	$0.50
BIG PRAWNS	$1.30
POTATO FLOUR	$0.70
SESAME SEEDS	$0.70
EGG FLOUR	$0.90
SHRIMPS	$1.30
FISH BALL	$0.70
FISH CAKE	$1.00
SOYA BEAN PEANUTS	$0.70
MIX VEGETABLES	$0.80
BEANCURD	$0.70
POTATO	BETWEEN SIZE

EGGS FLOUR · SESAME SEEDS · BIG PRAWNS & FLOUR

ED EGGS · FISHCAKE · POTATO & FLOUR · FISHBALL · SHRIMPS (CRISPY)

BEANCURD · CUTTLEFISH · POTATO

The Best Show in Town

Food centres—where
Singapore's famous hawker food lives on

Pages 20 & 21:
Indian Rojak,
a distinctive
Singapore Indian
version of a
Malay/Indonesian
snack, is a
dish you'd never
find in India.
Right:
Lau Pa Sat
Market, an
architectural
gem, is one of
the many food
centres where
Singapore's
astonishing
culinary diversity
can be enjoyed.

They once roamed the streets of Singapore, itinerant food hawkers who fed a mostly male populace too busy earning a living to cook for themselves. Today, hawkers no longer ply their trade in the streets, but have been re-located inside permanent food centres which most Singaporeans persist in calling hawker centres.

More than half of the women in Singapore work outside the home, and home-cooked meals are therefore something of a weekend event rather than daily necessity. Most people eat out at least once a day, and the top choice for a quick, tasty meal is the food centre or increasingly more upmarket air-conditioned food court.

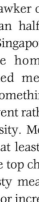

Food stalls are now permanent fixtures in a variety of places ranging from an open-air setting to covered markets and food centres, to air-conditioned food courts with more comfort and better decor.

The ubiquitous Chinese noodles were and still are the staples of any good food centre. Take your pick from rice, wheat, bean or soya noodles. They come thin, thick, flat, round or square, fresh, dried or fried in oil. You can have your noodles braised, stir-fried, tossed in spicy sauce mixtures or dunked in soup either plain or spicy. They also come in Chinese, Indian or Malay style.

However, the choice now stretches beyond noodles to rice with a variety of Chinese dishes, Malay or Indian curries, barbecued seafood, hamburgers, hot dogs, steaks and chops and even pizza. Even drinks go beyond the prosaic to delicious if plain-looking soya bean milk, downright exotic black grass herb jelly, freshly squeezed sugar cane juice or healthy fruit juices blended fresh from fruits on display. Familiar cow's milk becomes Susu Bandung, milk flavoured with rose syrup and coloured a garish pink.

Eating at a food centre involves all your senses. Your ears are assailed by the shouts of the cooks, the clatter and bang of ladles on giant woks or *kuali*; your nose twitches with every waft of fragrant steam from bubbling pots and *kualis* sitting over roaring fires. A reputation for good food or a convenient location make some food centres more popular than others, and if you come at peak hours, you may even had to stand over someone having his meal in order to get his table when he is done.

A food centre is not the place for elegant dining, but the no-frills approach does keep the cost of eating out low. And there are many Singaporeans who will swear that food at such places beats that dished out in some fancy restaurants. Certainly, the Char Kway Tiao (stir-fried rice noodles), Wan Tan Mee (noodles served with stuffed dumplings) and Mee Goreng (fried noodles) served up at many five-star hotel coffee houses are often poor imitations of the real thing to be found in the hot and noisy hawker centres or even the food courts where there is air-conditioning along with higher prices, but the food is not necessarily tastier.

This, may be why the Satay Club at Singapore's Esplanade continues to be a top draw with both visitors and locals. Here the tables are set under the stars and your friendly satay man sits on a low stool as he grills your sticks of satay nearby. You go home with your hair smelling of grilled meat, but nothing beats this meal of sticks of barbecued meat dipped in a spicy peanut gravy eaten in the cool

It doesn't matter whether it's an upmarket air-conditioned food court or an old, no-frills market such as Tiong Bahru. If the food is good, there'll always be an enthusiastic crowd.

darkness of the night, lit softly by lamps and the glow of coal fires all around. Unlike most other hawker centres with their predominance of Chinese food stalls, the Satay Club is a showcase not only of that Malay *piece de resistance*, satay, but also of other Indian and Malay stall food. Open only for dinner, the Satay Club is rare in still having the same open-air ambience that it has had for decades, even if on a larger, more varied scale.

Kopi Tiam

The inimitable Singaporean coffee shop

"Coffee shop talk" is a phrase Singaporeans use to describe gossip, and no wonder since the neighbourhood coffee shop or *kopi tiam* is where news, views and grouses are exchanged over a cup of coffee or a quick meal.

In a typical *kopi tiam*, the drinks stall is run by the owner who also sells such breakfast items as toast and butter, half-boiled eggs and small snacks. The other food comes from stallholders, often ethnically mixed to get variety, who lease space from the owner.

This water colour by Daniel Wegera captures the tranquil mood of the old-style kopi tiam, *as much a social centre as a place to eat and drink.*

In a decent *kopi tiam* of old, the owner roasted and ground his own beans, and some developed quite a reputation for their brew. Singapore coffee is thick and strong; roasted maize and margarine are often added, along with a dollop of syrupy thick sweetened condensed milk. So strong were these that stories circulated of how opium, once legal and easily available, was added to boost the potency of caffeine. Now most *kopi tiam* owners depend on coffee factories for their supplies.

In the mornings, the *kopi tiam* fills up with people eating breakfast, be it buttered toast sprinkled with white sugar or spread with *kaya* (egg and coconut) jam, or a bowl of noodles washed down with *kopi o* (black coffee) or coffee with condensed milk. In the late morning, the crowd thins out but there are always a few shift workers or senior citizens who linger over a cuppa for some "coffee shop talk".

Towards lunch time, children attending the afternoon session drift in for an early lunch before school, followed by those who have just finished the morning session. Part of the lunch crowd is made up of workers from nearby shops and offices. Afternoons are a little quiet until evening brings back people in search of dinner, then the diners give way to those who want to socialise over a beer or stout.

The ebb and flow of customers depends on the *kopi tiam*'s location and character. Some pack up by early evening, others only in the wee hours of the morning. The *kopi tiam*, despite competition from upmarket air-conditioned food centres and restaurants, is still the soul of Singapore.

Etiquette and Enjoyment

Share and share alike when eating Singapore style

Whatever the ethnic community in Singapore, eating is communal whether at home or in a restaurant. The assortment of dishes appear all at once, diners get individual servings of rice and then help themselves to the dishes using a serving spoon. One exception to this is the Chinese banquet, a formal eight or ten-course dinner, where the dishes appear one at a time.

"Don't use your fingers" is not an admonishment you will hear often. Indians, Malays and Straits Chinese will tell you that curry and rice taste best when you can literally feel the food with your fingers.

Eating with your hand has its own etiquette too. Only the right hand is used and just the tips of the fingers; the palm has to be kept perfectly clean. Washing the hands before eating is not only polite but more hygienic. In the finer Indian and Malay restaurants, a waiter will bring a bowl of warm water before and after a meal. In the more pedestrian curry shops or "banana leaf" restaurants , there will be a row of wash basins and soap for customers to clean up. Even with clean hands, diners should touch only the food on their plate, never that in the communal dishes, and the left hand is used to hold the serving spoon to keep it clean.

Chinese food is more likely to be eaten with chopsticks, although at some Chinese food stalls and in many Chinese homes, forks, spoons and plates are used. However, at a ten-course Chinese meal, chopsticks are *de rigueur*. Sucking or licking the tips of the chopsticks is impolite and contact between mouth and the tips is kept minimal. Spoons are set out for larger mouthfuls. Often before and always at the end of the meal, hot towels are handed round for cleaning the face and hands.

Although Chinese tea is the traditional drink with Chinese food, there is nothing quite like beer to take the heat off your tongue and to cool you down when you eat spicy food. One of the major local beers, Tiger, has won awards world-wide and has even been immortalised in Anthony Burgess' satirical novel, *Time for a Tiger.*

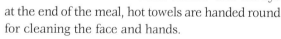

Ordering and enjoying a Chinese meal is easy, especially with menus in English and prices clearly displayed in food centres such as the revived Bugis Street area.

Part Two: The Singapore Kitchen

All modern appliances gratefully accepted

At first glance, the typical Singapore kitchen is like its counterpart in any Western country: modern, with tiled floors, electrical appliances and the refrigerator so essential in a tropical climate.

Look a little closer, however, and you'll find a number of subtle differences. Not all kitchens, for example, have cookers complete with an oven, as most cooking is done on the top of a stove. Electric mini-ovens used for grilling and toasting are, however, increasingly making their way into Singapore kitchens. **Gas** is preferred for simmering, frying and steaming, as the heat can be quickly adjusted. It is worth noting that very high heat is required for stir frying Chinese dishes and for heating oil for deep frying.

Almost every Singapore kitchen has an **electric rice cooker**, which guarantees soft, fluffy rice every time and keeps rice warm for any late-comers. Although a rice cooker is not essential, you'll find it a great help if you eat rice fairly often.

Saucepans are normally of enamel or stainless steel; aluminium is best avoided, especially for dishes containing tamarind or other acidic ingredients. Traditional cooks still insist on Chinese **claypots** or unglazed **earthenware pots** (often known by their Malay name, *belangah*), for certain dishes. These are generally inexpensive as well as attractive, and often available in Asian specialty shops overseas.

Essential for all types of Singaporean food, the conical **wok** is known locally by its Malay name, *kuali*. A wok has to be the best designed, multi-purpose kitchen utensil anywhere. When food is tossed about during stir-frying, the sloping sides ensure that the food falls back into the wok and not outside, while less oil is required for deep frying. For dishes requiring a considerable reduction of the sauce, the wide wok allows the correct amount of evaporation. If you use an electric rather than gas fire, try to find a flat-bottomed wok. Always choose the heaviest wok you can find; cast iron, once the preferred material, is increasingly being replaced by various alloys.

Although various type of **steamer** are available, even here the wok holds its own. A perforated metal disc which sits about two-thirds of the way up inside the wok above boiling water is used for

Opposite:
Time-saving devices are standard in the modern Singapore kitchen.
Left:
Rice cookers are found in almost every home.
Above:
High-tech alloys now replace cast iron as the favourite material for the wok.

and pestle on hand for quick pounding of small amounts of various spices and seasonings. Although acknowledging that this age-old method gets a better result, most modern cooks prefer the speed and ease of an **electric blender** for grinding dried spices as well as large amounts of seasonings for the spice paste or *rempah* that is the basis of many dishes.

PREPARING A SPICE PASTE

Whether you are using a mortar and pestle or a blender or food processor to prepare the spice paste or *rempah* used in many Singaporean dishes, you should follow certain rules. All ingredients should be chopped or sliced first. The hardest ingredients (such as galangal and lemon grass) should be processed until fine before adding softer ingredients like shallots, chillies and ginger. Shrimp paste should be added at the last moment and processed just to mix well. Dried spices should be ground separately from the "wet" spices mentioned above.

When using a blender or food processor, you may need to add a little liquid to keep the blades turning. If the *rempah* is to be fried, add a spoonful or two of the specified amount of cooking oil, while if it is to be simmered in coconut milk or stock, add some of this instead.

Above:
Modern materials are increasingly used for mesh baskets, and frying scoops or shovels.
Below right:
Although most cooks believe a mortar and pestle is better, the quick and easy-to-use blender is now favoured for grinding spice pastes.

holding plates of food; the wok is then covered with a large domed lid. A woven **bamboo steaming basket**, aesthetically appealing as well as practical, is designed to be set inside a wok; the bamboo absorbs any moisture during steaming, preventing it from falling back onto the food. If using a metal steamer, put a folded towel under the lid to absorb moisture.

Singapore's Indian kitchens have traditionally used a heavy iron **griddle** or *tawa* for cooking Chapati, Dosai and other breads, although some modern cooks prefer to use a large non-stick frying pan for such tasks.

A flat **frying shovel** or spatula is used for stir frying in a wok, while **wire-mesh baskets** (traditionally made of brass with a bamboo handle) are ideal for lifting deep-fried food out of the wok, or for removing noodles from boiling water.

A large, heavy wooden **chopping board** partnered by a strong **cleaver** with a blade about 8–10 cm (3–4 in) deep are indispensable for cutting up poultry, crabs and fish, for chopping vegetables and for mincing fish or meats to the desired texture.

Most Singapore cooks keep a granite **mortar**

Singapore Ingredients

Spices, seasonings, sauces and
a host of other goodies from both East and West

Where they can be of assistance in identification, local names are given in either Malay (M), Hokkien (H), Cantonese (C) or Tamil (T).

AGAR AGAR: A setting agent made from seaweed, which sets without refrigeration. It comes in long strands or in powder form; 1 teaspoon of powder sets about 1–1½ cups liquid.

AUBERGINE (M: *terong*, T: *brinjal*): Most of the aubergines (eggplants) used in Singapore are the slender purple-skinned variety about 15–20 cm (6–8 in) long. Unlike European aubergines, Asian varieties are not bitter and do not need salting before use.

BAMBOO SHOOTS: Fresh bamboo shoots must first be peeled, sliced and simmered for about 30 minutes until tender. If using canned bamboo shoots, try to find winter bamboo shoots, which are sweetest; remove any metallic taste by boiling in fresh water for a couple of minutes. Can be refrigerated for about a week covered in water, which should be changed every couple of days.

BEANCURD: Rich in protein and amazingly versatile, various types of beancurd, originally introduced by the Chinese, are now used by almost every ethnic group in Singapore. **Soft white beancurd** (C: *tau foo*) is often steamed or added to soups, while **hard squares of beancurd** (*tau kwa*) are often deep fried. Small cubes of **dried deep-fried beancurd** (*tau foo pok*) are added to slow-cooked dishes and some soups. **Pickled bean curd** (*nam yee*), sold in jars and either red or white in colour, is used in small amounts as a seasoning in Chinese dishes.

BEANSPROUTS (C: *taugeh*): Sprouted green mung peas are eaten blanched in some salads and soups, or quickly stir-fried as a vegetable dish. They can be stored in a refrigerator for 2–3 days, if covered with water which is changed daily.

BROWN MUSTARD SEED (M: *biji sawi*): A small round brown seed used in many southern Indian dishes. Do not substitute it with common yellow mustard seed, as the flavour is different.

CANDLENUT (M: *buah keras*): A waxy, cream-coloured nut similar in size and shape to a macadamia nut, which can be used as a substitute (although less expensive almonds or cashews will also do). It is never eaten raw, but ground and cooked with other seasonings in some Malay and Nonya dishes.

CARDAMOM (T: *elakai*, M: *buah pelaga*): Straw-coloured pods containing about 8–10 tiny black seeds with an intense fragrance, these are used in Indian as well as some Malay dishes.

CELERY, CHINESE (H: *kin chye*): Often referred to as "Chinese" or "local" celery, this is much smaller than the western variety, and has a very intense flavour. The leaves and sometimes the stems are used as a herb rather than a vegetable, added to soups, some rice dishes and stir-fried vegetables. Chinese celery is often obtainable in Asian speciality stores; substitute regular celery if not available.

CHILLI: Both fresh and dried chillies are used. Large, finger-length green (unripe) and red (ripe) chillies are moderately hot. **Dried red chillies** of this variety are usually cut or broken in 2.5 cm (1 in) lengths, soaked in warm water to soften and pounded to add heat to many dishes. The flavour of fresh and dried chillies is different, so be sure to use the type specified in the recipes. Tiny red, green or yellowy-orange **bird's-eye chillies** (M: *cili padi*) used in some dishes or *sambals* (condiments) are very hot.

CHILLI SAUCE: Many different types of commercially bottled chilli sauce are available, and placed on the table to spike up countless dishes. Some varieties add garlic, some are fairly acid and others distinctly sweet. Brands from different Asian countries vary considerably, so try to find one made in either Singapore or Malaysian for a genuinely local flavour.

CHINESE SAUSAGE (C: *lap cheong*): Mottled reddish sausages with a high fat content and delicately perfumed with rice wine, these are used as a seasoning rather than being eaten on their own like European sausages. Sold in pairs, they keep almost indefinitely without refrigeration.

CHINESE WINE: Used as a seasoning in many Chinese dishes; dry sherry can be used as a substitute.

CLOVES: The whole, nail-shaped spice (not clove powder) is used in some Malay and Indian dishes.

COARSE CHIVES (H: *koo chye*): More like flattened spring onions than the very fine round western chives, these chives have an emphatic garlic flavour and are often added to noodle or stir-fried vegetable dishes during the final stages of cooking. A delicate blanched variety is cooked as a vegetable.

COCONUT MILK: The flesh of mature coconuts is grated and squeezed without water to make coconut cream. To obtain thick coconut milk, about $\frac{1}{2}$ cup of water is added for each coconut, then squeezed and strained. Thin coconut milk is obtained by adding a further 2 cups of water to the already squeezed coconut. Unless otherwise specified, "coconut milk" in this book is a combination of both thick and thin milks. Various substitutes may be obtained overseas; canned coconut cream, which should be diluted according to instructions, or powdered coconut which is mixed with water, are the most acceptable.

CORIANDER: Sprigs of fresh coriander leaf (sometimes known as cilantro overseas) are widely used as a garnish for Chinese dishes, and add an inimitable fragrance. Fortunately, this herb is increasingly widely available and can easily be grown in a pot at home. Small round coriander seeds (M: *ketumbar*), with their faintly orangey smell, are one of the most frequently used ingredients in both Malay and Indian spice blends.

CUMIN (M: *jintan putih*): This spice, which looks similar to caraway, is frequently partnered with coriander in basic spice mixtures. Don't confuse it with the more fragrant fennel, which looks similar but is whiter and slightly fatter.

CURRY LEAF (T: *karuvapillai*, M: *daun kari*): Sprigs of these small, dark green leaves are widely used by Southern Indian cooks in Singapore; other ethnic groups also use them in fish curries. Do not substitute with bay leaves or the Indonesian *daun salam*, as sometimes suggested, as the flavour is totally different. Dried curry leaves are sometimes available.

CURRY POWDER: Various blends of spices are ground together to form curry powders. Certain spice combinations are appropriate to different basic foods, and curry powders labelled "Fish", "Meat", "Chicken" and other more specific dishes such as "Korma", "Rendang" etc. should be used for that particular purpose only. If you use a meat curry powder for a fish dish, for example, the final flavour will not be harmonious. Curry powders are often blended with water to a stiff paste before being fried, so that less oil is needed. For maximum freshness, store curry powder in a jar in the deep freeze.

FENNEL (M: *jintan manis*): This spice, similar in appearance to cumin, smells strongly of aniseed, and adds a sweet fragrance to a number of Malay and Indian dishes.

FIVE-SPICE POWDER (C: *ng heong fun*): A blend of spices including cinnamon, cloves, fennel, Sichuan pepper and ginger used in some Chinese dishes.

FRAGRANT LIME (M: *limau purut*): Sometimes known as kaffir lime, this citrus fruit has a very knobbly and intensely fragrant skin, but virtually no juice. Fragrant lime leaves (*daun limau purut*) are also used in soups or liquid dishes and curries of Malay or Nonya origin.

GALANGAL (M: *lengkuas*): A rhizome similar to ginger in appearance, this adds a wonderful flavour to many Malay and Nonya dishes. Slices of dried galangal (sometimes sold under the Indonesian name, *laos*) must be soaked in boiling water for about 30 minutes until softened. Jars of tender, sliced galangal packed in water are exported from Thailand and make an adequate substitute for the fresh root.

GARLIC: Garlic cloves are often much smaller in Southeast Asia than in Western countries, so use your discretion when following amounts given in the recipes.

GINGELLY OIL: Light oil made from unroasted sesame seeds, this is quite different in flavour from Chinese sesame oil. It adds a distinctive touch to Indian pickles.

GINGER: Use only fresh ginger, as dried powdered ginger has a completely different flavour. The young variety, which is pale yellow with a pinkish tinge, is juicier than the more mature ginger, which has a light brown skin that should be scraped off before use. Pickled ginger, available in jars, is mild yet flavourful, and is an essential accompaniment to several Chinese dishes.

KALE: Known in Singapore by its Cantonese name, *kai lan*, this vegetable is enjoyed for its firm texture and emphatic flavour. Only the tender portions of the stems are used, generally peeled and halved lengthwise if they are thick. Broccoli stems are a good substitute. **Baby *kai lan***, a recently de-

veloped vegetable grown by crowding the plants together and force-feeding them, is cooked whole.

LAKSA LEAF (M: *daun kesum*): This pungent, dark green leaf (*Polygonum hydropiper*) is sometimes called "Vietnamese mint" overseas. There is no substitute.

LEMON GRASS (M: *serai*): A lemon-scented grass, which grows in clumps and adds a delightful aroma to many Malay and Nonya dishes. Each plant resembles a miniature leek. Use only the bottom 10–15 cm (4–6 in) of the lemon grass, and if it is to be pounded or blended to a paste, peel off several of the outer leaves to get the tender centre of the plant. Dried lemon grass is sometimes available overseas; another substitute is powdered lemon grass (sometimes sold under the Indonesian name, *sereh*). About 1 teaspoon equals one whole plant.

LIME: Three types are lime are used in Singapore. The largest lime, which is about the size of a small egg with a greenish-yellow skin, has a tart flavour similar to lemons, which can be used as a substitute. **Small round green limes** (M: *limau kesturi*) about the size of a walnut have a less acidic, more fragrant

juice, and are preferred for squeezing over many cooked noodle dishes and into the ubiquitous Sambal Belacan. They are sometimes available under their Filipino name, *kalamansi*. (Fragrant or kaffir limes are described on page 31.)

MUSHROOMS, DRIED BLACK: Dried black mushrooms, which should be soaked in warm water for 15–20 minutes to soften before cooking, have a completely different flavour to the fresh variety and are available in Asian speciality shops abroad.

NOODLES: A universal favourite in Singapore, which the Malays, Nonyas and Indians have enthusiastically adopted from the Chinese. Both fresh and dried noodles made from either wheat flour, rice flour or mung pea flour are sold. The most popular types are: **fresh yellow** or **"Hokkien" noodles**, heavy spaghetti-like noodles made from flour and egg, used by Chinese cooks and also by Malays for Mee Rebus and Indians for their famous Indian Mee Goreng; **dried wheat-flour noodles** (H: *mee*), prepared in countless ways after being plunged into boiling water to soften; **fresh flat rice-flour noodles** (C: *sa hor fun*, H: *kway teow*), ribbon-like noodles about 1 cm (½in) wide, used in soups or fried; **fresh laksa noodles**, which look like white spaghetti and are used in the popular laksa noodle soup; **dried rice-flour vermicelli** (C: *meehoon*; H: *beehoon*), sometimes known as rice-stick noodles abroad; **dried mung pea noodles** (C: *sohoon*, H: *tanghoon*), fine white strands, generally used in

soups and sometimes referred to as "glass", "jelly" or "transparent" noodles, all accurate descriptions of their appearance after soaking.

OYSTER SAUCE: Most brands of oyster sauce contain monosodium glutamate to intensify the flavour of the dish to which they are added. Particularly popular splashed over stir-fried vegetable dishes during the last stage of cooking.

PALM SUGAR (M: *gula Melaka*): Made from the sap of coconut palms or the *aren* (sugar palm) tree, so-called "Malacca" sugar is sold in solid cakes or cylinders and varies in colour from gold to light brown. If not available, use soft brown sugar or white cane sugar with a touch of maple or golden syrup. Make **palm sugar syrup** by boiling together equal quantities of chopped sugar and water.

PANDAN LEAF (M: *daun pandan*): A fragrant member of the pandanus or screwpine family, pandan leaf is used as a wrapping for seasoned morsels of chicken or pork rib and added to various cakes and desserts.

PRAWNS, DRIED (C: *hay bee*): Small dried prawns or shrimps are a popular seasoning, particularly in sauces, condiments (*sambals*) and vegetable dishes. They should be soaked in warm water for about 5 minutes to soften before use.

PLUM SAUCE: A sweet Chinese sauce made from plums, vinegar, sugar and a touch of chillies. Available in jars or cans in any Chinese store.

RADISH, GIANT WHITE (C: *lobak*): A vegetable about 15–25 cm (6–10 in) long, widely used in Japanese cooking (and known as *daikon*); sometimes referred to as "white carrot" in Singapore, it is eaten both raw and cooked.

RICE: All Singapore's rice is imported, the most popular being the fragrant long-grain Thai rice. **White glutinous rice** (M: *pulot*) and a **purplish-black glutinous rice** with a nutty flavour are used to make cakes and desserts. Some Northern Indian dishes are best prepared with fragrant **Basmati rice**, which has a thin, beige-coloured grain. The absorbency of rice is affected by its age, with young rice absorbing less water than older rice. When you use a new packet of rice, be conservative when adding water until you find out its degree of absorbency.

SALTED CABBAGE (C: *ham choy*, H: *kiam chye*): Various types of heavily salted cabbage are used in some Chinese and Nonya dishes. Soak in fresh water for at least 15 minutes to remove excess saltiness, repeating if necessary.

SALTED EGG: Salted duck eggs are used as a side dish with Malay meals. The eggs should be boiled for about 10 minutes before being peeled. They are sometimes covered with a thick layer of black soil to protect them during transportation; this should be rubbed off before boiling.

SALTED FISH : Several varieties of salted dried fish are used, mainly as a seasoning or condiment. They are not soaked in water before using but sliced and fried to a crisp. Salted fish is sometimes made into a pickle.

SALTED SOYA BEANS (H: *tau cheo*): Salty and with a distinctive tang, these are often lightly pounded before being used to season some fish, noodle or vegetable dishes. Varieties exported from China are sometimes confusingly labelled "Yellow Bean Sauce"; while there are also brands which add sugar to already ground beans.

SESAME OIL (C: *ma yau*): Added to some Chinese dishes—usually at the last minute—for seasoning, but never used on its own as a frying medium.

SHALLOTS (M: *bawang merah*): Small round pinkish-purple shallots add a sweet oniony flavour to countless dishes, and are also sliced, deep fried and used as a garnish.

SHRIMP PASTE : Many different types of **dried shrimp paste** (M: *belacan*), ranging in colour from pink to blackish-brown, are available. Shrimp paste should always be cooked before eating. If the recipe calls for it to be toasted, wrap in a piece of foil and cook in a dry pan or under a grill for about 2 minutes, turn and cook another 2 minutes. **Black shrimp paste** (H: *hay koh*) is a pungent, treacle-like substance used in Rojak and Penang-style noodle soups.

SOY SAUCE: **Light soy sauce** is saltier and paler in colour than the **dark black** variety; as both have their characteristic flavour, be sure to use the type specified when following these recipes. **Sweet soy sauce** is used in a few dishes of Indonesian origin;

if this is not available, use black soy sauce with a little brown sugar.

SPRING ONION: Used as a herb, a vegetable and a garnish; sometimes known as green onions, scallions or, rather confusingly, as shallots in Australia.

STAR ANISE: A dark brown spice, like an 8-pointed star, with a pungent aniseed flavour; used in both Chinese and Malay cooking.

SWEET SAUCE (C: *tim cheong*): Several types of sweet sauce, usually sold in jars, are available. **Black sweet sauce** is somewhat treacly, and completely different from the **red sweet sauce** used in some marinades and sauces.

TAMARIND (M: *asam*): Dried tamarind pulp is soaked in water for 5 minutes then squeezed and strained to obtain the sour, fragrant juice. If using already cleaned tamarind pulp or concentrate, reduce the amounts called for in these recipes. Slices of a sour dried fruit, *asam gelugor*, are sometimes used instead of tamarind pulp.

TURMERIC: A member of the ginger family, this rhizome has a very rich yellow interior (which can stain clothing and plastic utensils) and a pleasant pungency which is absent in dried turmeric powder. The former is generally preferred in Singapore; substitute ½ teaspoon turmeric powder to 1 cm (½in) fresh turmeric.

WATER CHESTNUT: Although it is troublesome to peel the dark brown skin of this crunchy tuber, it's well worth using fresh water chestnuts if you can find them. They are excellent in salads and often added to stir-fried vegetable dishes. Fresh yam bean is a better substitute for fresh water chestnuts than the canned variety.

VINEGAR: Distilled white vinegar is the type to use for most Singaporean recipes. Exceptions are **Chinese black** or **red rice vinegar**, both of which have a distinctive flavour and are not interchangeable.

WATER CONVOLVULUS (M: *kangkung*): This aquatic plant, a member of the convolvulus or morning glory family, is an excellent-tasting vegetable full of nutrition. It is sometimes known as swamp cabbage or water spinach. The leaves and tender tips are usually stir-fried. Discard the tough, hollow stems.

YAM BEAN (M: *bengkuang*): Known as *jicama* in the Americas, where it originated, this crunchy, mild tuber has a white interior and beige skin, which peels off easily.

Part Three: The Recipes

Recipes for pickles, sambals and condiments
precede those for the main dishes, which begin on page 42

In Singapore homes and restaurants, several dishes are presented together on the table, allowing diners to serve themselves to whatever they want. As a general rule, these recipes will serve 4–6 people as part of a meal with rice and 2–3 other dishes.

PICKLES

Mango Pickle

10 unripe green mangoes, weighing a total of about 2 kg (4 lb)
½ cup gingelly oil
1 teaspoon mustard seeds

Marinade:
2 tablespoons chilli powder
1 teaspoon turmeric powder
3 tablespoons salt
1 teaspoon distilled white vinegar

Peel the mangoes and cut into small dice. Mix together the marinade ingredients, add the mangoes, mix well and marinate for three days.

Heat the oil in a wok or a heavy saucepan, then add mustard seeds and marinated mango. Sauté, stirring constantly, for 3–4 minutes. Remove from fire and allow to cool. Store in glass jars in the refrigerator for up to 1 month.

Measurements

Measurements in this book are given in volume as far as possible: 1 measuring **cup** contains 250 ml (roughly 8 oz); 1 **teaspoon** contains 5 ml, while 1 **tablespoon** contains 15 ml or the equivalent of 3 teaspoons. Australian readers please note that the standard Australian measuring spoon is larger, containing 20 ml or 4 teaspoons, so use only ¾ tablespoon when following the recipes. Where metric measurements are given, approximate imperial conversions follow in brackets.

Time Estimates

Time estimates for preparation only (excluding cooking) are based on the assumption that a food processor or blender will be used.

🕐 *quick and very easy to prepare*

🕐🕐 *relatively easy; less than 15 minutes' preparation*

🕐🕐🕐 *takes more than 15 minutes to prepare*

Opposite:Clockwise from top: Mango Pickle, Lime Pickle and Acar Kuning (Vegetable Pickle).

Lime Pickles

10 large green limes
3 tablespoons salt
$\frac{1}{2}$ cup gingelly oil
2 teaspoons mustard seed
4 cloves garlic, sliced
3 cm ($1\frac{1}{4}$ in) ginger, sliced
1 tablespoon coriander powder
1 tablespoon chilli powder
1 teaspoon fennel
1 teaspoon cumin
1 teaspoon turmeric powder
10 curry leaves

Put the whole limes into a bowl, cover with boiling water and leave to stand for 20 minutes. Drain, cut each lime into 8 pieces and rub with the salt. Put in a glass jar with a lid and leave in the sun for at least two hours a day for a minimum of 6 days to "cure" the limes.

Heat the oil and fry the mustard seeds until they begin to pop. Add garlic, ginger and all other ingredients and cook gently for two minutes. Add the limes and any liquid that may have accumulated and cook over very low heat, stirring from time to time, for 45–60 minutes. Can be kept in a covered jar for several months.

Acar Kuning • *Pickled Vegetables*

600 g ($1\frac{1}{4}$ lb) carrots
600 g ($1\frac{1}{4}$ lb) giant white radish
600 g ($1\frac{1}{4}$ lb) cucumbers
$\frac{1}{2}$ cup coarse salt
10 cloves garlic
5 cm (2 in) ginger
5 cm (2 in) turmeric
$\frac{1}{2}$ cup oil

2 lemon grass, bruised
30 shallots, deep fried whole
30 cloves garlic, deep fried whole
30 green bird's-eye chillies
1 teaspoon white pepper powder
2 tablespoons sugar
$\frac{1}{2}$ cup distilled white vinegar
3 cups water

Peel the carrots and radish and cut into strips 1 cm x 0.5 cm ($\frac{1}{2}$ x $\frac{1}{4}$ in), about 4 cm ($1\frac{1}{2}$ in) in length. Do not peel the cucumber but halve lengthwise, remove seeds and cut into the same size as the carrots and radish. Mix vegetables with salt and set aside for about 20 minutes while preparing the remaining ingredients.

Chop then pound or blend the 10 cloves garlic, ginger and turmeric until fine. Heat oil in heavy pan and add blended mixture, lemon grass, whole shallots, garlic and bird's-eye chillies. Sauté for 5 minutes over a low fire.

Add the prepared vegetables and stir thoroughly until well mixed. Add pepper, sugar and season to taste with salt. Add the vinegar and water and simmer for 3–4 minutes until the vegetables are just cooked but still firm. Set aside to cool. Can be stored in a covered jar in the refrigerator for up to 1 month.

SAMBALS

Chilli Sambal

10 bird's-eye chillies
20 red chillies
10 cloves garlic
$\frac{1}{2}$ cup oil
2 tablespoons concentrated tomato paste

Below:
Chilli Sambal

1 tablespoon dried prawns, soaked and
   pounded or blended
5 tablespoons lime juice from small round
   limes (*limau kesturi*) if possible
1 tablespoon sugar
salt and pepper to taste

Chop then pound or blend the chillies and garlic to obtain a fine paste, using a little of the oil to keep the blades turning. Heat remaining oil in a heavy saucepan and add the blended ingredients, tomato paste and dried prawns. Cook over low heat, stirring frequently, for about 5 minutes. Add lime juice and sugar, then season to taste with salt and pepper. Remove from the fire and allow to cool. Can be stored up to 2 weeks in a covered jar in the refrigerator.

Sambal Belacan • *Shrimp Paste Sambal*

10 red chillies
10 shallots
2 tomatoes, skins left on
2 tablespoons dried shrimp paste (*belacan*),
   toasted
3 tablespoons lime juice
1 teaspoon sugar
$1/2$ teaspoon salt

Chop all ingredients then pound or blend together to obtain a sauce. Serve together with halved small round limes (*limau kesturi*). Keeps covered in the refrigerator for about 1 week.

Chilli Ginger Sauce

100 g ($3^{1}/_{2}$ oz) red chillies
30 g (1 oz) garlic
30 g (1 oz) ginger
1 tablespoon white vinegar

1–2 teaspoons sugar
$1/2$ teaspoon salt

Chop then pound or blend all ingredients together to obtain a sauce. Serve with noodles and Chinese dishes. Can be stored in a covered container in the refrigerator for about 1 week.

Dried Prawn Sambal

20 red chillies
10 dried chillies, soaked until soft
10 bird's-eye chillies (optional)
2 tablespoons dried shrimp paste (*belacan*)
5 tablespoons dried prawns, soaked and
   blended until fine
8 shallots
6 cloves garlic
1 tablespoon concentrated tomato paste
$1/2$ cup oil
salt and sugar to taste

Chop and all ingredients except oil, salt and sugar, adding a little of the oil if necessary to keep the blades turning. Heat remaining oil and gently fry Add salt and sugar to taste. If like, any excess oil can be discarded before serving. Keeps covered in the refrigerator for up to 1 week.

MISCELLANEOUS

Ginger Juice

125 g (4 oz) fresh ginger
   (young ginger if
   possible)
5 tablespoons water

Scrape the skin off the ginger, chop coarsely and put in a blender

Below:
Chilli Ginger
Sauce

with water. Process until very fine. Strain through a sieve, pushing down with the back of a spoon to extract all the juice. This should provide about $\frac{1}{2}$ cup ginger juice, which can be stored in a refrigerator for up to 1 week.

Preserved Chinese Cabbage

500 g (1 lb) long white Chinese cabbage
500 g (1 lb) giant white radish
125 g (4 oz) carrot
$\frac{1}{2}$ cup coarse salt

Marinade:

5 red chillies
5 cloves garlic
$\frac{1}{2}$ cup ginger juice (page 39)
$\frac{1}{2}$ cup sesame seeds
$2\frac{1}{2}$ tablespoons sesame oil
1 cup water
2 tablespoons chilli powder
$\frac{1}{4}$ cup light soy sauce

Dried Prawn Sambal (left) and Sambal Belacan (right)

Separate the individual leaves of the cabbage and cut in thin slices. Peel the radish and cut in very fine lengthwise slices, using a vegetable peeler or food processor. Peel the carrot and cut into matchsticks. Marinate the Chinese cabbage and white radish with salt for about 1 day until all the water comes out. Squeeze the water out and rinse thoroughly with water.

To prepare the **marinade**, chop then pound or blend the chillies and garlic until fine. Mix with all the other marinade ingredients in a bowl. Place a layer of Chinese cabbage on a tray, cover with a little of the marinade then put on a layer of radish.

Cover with marinade, then repeat for the carrots. Repeat until all the ingredients are used up. Roll up the layered vegetables and slice crosswise with a knife to make rolls about 4 cm ($1\frac{1}{2}$ in) wide. Put in a jar, cover firmly and keep refrigerated for at least two days before serving. Can be kept up to 1 month.

Popiah Wrappers

185 g (6 oz) rice flour
20 g ($\frac{3}{4}$ oz) plain flour
$\frac{1}{2}$ teaspoon salt
4 eggs
1 teaspoon oil
2 cups water
$\frac{1}{2}$ teaspoon salt

Sift both types of flour and salt into a bowl. Mix eggs, oil and water together and stir into the dried ingredients, mixing until smooth. Leave in the refrigerator for a minimum of 1 hour. Cook in a non-stick pan, greasing it with the minimum amount of oil to stop the batter from sticking. Pour in just a little batter, swirl the pan to make a very thin pancake and cook on one side only over moderate heat until set. Put on a plate and repeat until the batter is used up. This makes about 20–25 *popiah* skins.

Chicken Stock

2 large mature hens or chickens, each cut in 4
5 litres (20 cups) water
8 cm (3 in) ginger, crushed
2 leeks, sliced

1 large onion, halved
1 carrot, diced
5 stalks Chinese celery (with leaves)

Wash hens well then blanch in the boiling water to cover for 3 minutes. Remove hens and discard water. Bring 5 litres fresh water to the boil with the chicken and vegetables. Simmer uncovered over low heat for 2–3 hours. This makes 3–4 litres of stock, which can be divided into smaller portions and stored in the deep-freeze.

Fried Shallots & Garlic

24 shallots or 10–15 cloves garlic
1 cup oil

Peel and slice the shallots or garlic finely, and dry well with a paper towel. Heat the oil and deep fry the shallots or garlic until golden brown and crisp. Take care not to let them burn or the flavour will be bitter. Drain and cool completely before storing. Keep **shallot** or **garlic oil** and use for frying or seasoning other dishes.

Char Siew • Red Roasted Pork

This is often used with Chinese noodle dishes, in fried rice and as a stuffing in steamed buns (*pow*).

600 g pork belly (part meat, part fat), or
    pork fillet if less fat preferred
$\frac{1}{2}$ cup sugar
4 tablespoons light soy sauce
2 tablespoons black soy sauce
1 tablespoon red food colouring
1 teaspoon five-spice powder
1 teaspoon sesame oil
1 teaspoon Chinese wine

Marinate the pork with remaining ingredients, first mixed well in a bowl, for about 1 hour. Roast on a wire rack in a moderately hot oven (200°C/400°F) for about 30 minutes. Leave to cool and slice only when needed. Can be refrigerated for several days.

Flour Crisps

125 g (4 oz) plain flour
2 teaspoons butter
$\frac{1}{2}$ teaspoon oil
$\frac{1}{2}$ teaspoon salt
1 egg
5 shallots blended with 3 cloves garlic

Mix all ingredients together to make a dough. Roll as thin as possible and cut into small squares. Deep fry in very hot oil and store in an airtight container.

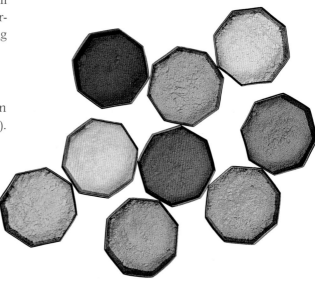

Ground spices not only add flavour to many Singapore dishes but are attractive to look at as well.

POPIAH

Hokkien-style Fresh Spring Roll

A tasty snack which can also be served as part of a main meal, Hokkien *popiah* are normally made with very thin fresh wrappers made from flour and water. If you are not able to obtain fresh *popiah* skins or the similar Filipino *lumpia* wrappers, follow the recipe for *popiah* skins on page 40. ☺ ☺

> **6 *popiah* wrappers**
> **1 red chilli, sliced, or 4 red chillies pounded to a paste with a little salt**
> **2 shallots, finely chopped**
> **1 teaspoon pounded garlic**
> **1 tablespoon sweet black sauce (*tim cheong*)**

Filling:

> **1 tablespoon oil**
> **1 yam bean, peeled and shredded**
> **4 shallots, sliced**
> **pinch of five-spice powder**
> **$\frac{1}{2}$ teaspoon salt**
> **6 lettuce leaves**
> **60 g (2 oz) beansprouts**
> **60 g (2 oz) crabmeat**
> **12 medium-sized cooked prawns, peeled and halved lengthwise**
> **1 hard-boiled egg, halved lengthwise then sliced across**
> **1 Chinese sausage (*lap cheong*), sliced and blanched in hot water**

Prepare the **filling** by sautéing the yam bean and shallots in oil for about 5 minutes, until soft. Season with five-spice powder and salt and leave to cool.

To stuff the *popiah*, lay a skin flat on a plate or board. Smear with a little of the black sauce and pounded garlic, then smear with chilli paste or sprinkle with sliced chilli and shallots. Lay a lettuce leaf on top and add one-sixth of the beansprouts, crabmeat, prawns, egg, Chinese sausage and cooked yam bean. Tuck in the sides and roll up the *popiah* firmly. Repeat for remaining 5 *popiah*. Cut each *popiah* across in 4–5 pieces before serving.

ROAST DUCK AND ROCK MELON SALAD

Roast duck has always been considered fit for festive occasions and banquet dinners. This modern adaptation shows the Western influence in the partnering of fruit with the duck. ☺☺☺

1 fresh duck, about 2 kg (4 lb)
1 ripe rock melon, in balls

Seasoning:

2 tablespoons salted soya beans (*tau cheo*), mashed
4 whole star anise
1 cinnamon stick (8 cm/3 in long)
1 tablespoon light soy sauce
¹⁄₂ teaspoon black soy sauce
1 tablespoon sugar
2 tablespoons sweet red sauce (*tim cheong*)
1 teaspoon sesame oil
red food colouring

For Blanching:

2 litres (8 cups) water
1 cup Chinese red vinegar
1 cup Chinese wine
2 large limes or lemons, sliced
3 tablespoons glucose syrup or corn syrup

Sauce:

4 tablespoons sour plum sauce
3 tablespoons light salad oil
1 teaspoon sesame oil
1 cup rock melon juice (obtained by blending the melon left over after extracting the balls)

Wash and dry the duck thoroughly. Mix **seasoning** ingredients in a bowl and then put inside the duck. Close the duck with a satay stick or small skewer.

Bring **blanching** ingredients to the boil in a large pan. Hold the duck firmly in one hand and use a ladle in the other to pour the water over the duck for about 1 minute. Rub duck skin with red food colouring. Hang up the duck in an airy space or under the sun for at least 2 hours to dry the skin thoroughly.

When the duck is dry, put it in a hot oven and roast for about 45 minutes. Allow to cool. Before serving, debone the duck and cut in slices.

Combine the **sauce** ingredients, stirring to mix well. To serve, arrange the duck slices and melon balls on a plate and pour over the sauce.

Helpful hints: There are two types of Chinese vinegar, one almost black in colour (often referred to as Tienstin vinegar) and the other a light reddish brown. The flavour is quite different, so be sure to use the latter for this dish. To save time, you can buy red-roasted Chinese duck from a Chinese supply shop or market.

TEA-SMOKED SEABASS

Smoking food—especially duck—over a mixture of tea leaves is a popular method of preparing food in Yunnan and Sichuan provinces in China. This excellent Singapore adaptation makes use of the abundant supply of seafood found locally. ☯☯

1 whole seabass fillet, about 500–600 g
(1–1¼ lb), or other firm white fish fillet
such as snapper or garoupa
5 tablespoons Chinese black tea leaves
5 star anise
3 cinnamon sticks (about 8 cm/3 in long)
20 cloves
5 tablespoons raw rice
5 cloves garlic, crushed

Marinade:
2 cups iced water
5 tablespoons soy sauce
1 tablespoon sugar
½ cup ginger juice (page 39)
2 tablespoons salt

Mix the marinade, put in the fish and leave for about 3 hours. Remove the seabass from the marinade, drain, dry with paper towels and set aside.

Heat a wok over a low fire and put in the remaining ingredients. Put the fish on wire grill or round bamboo rack inside the wok at least 5 cm (2 in) above the smoking ingredients. Cover the wok and smoke over a low fire for 10–15 minutes, until the fish has turned brown and is cooked through.

Slice and serve either hot or cold with Preserved Chinese Cabbage (page 40).

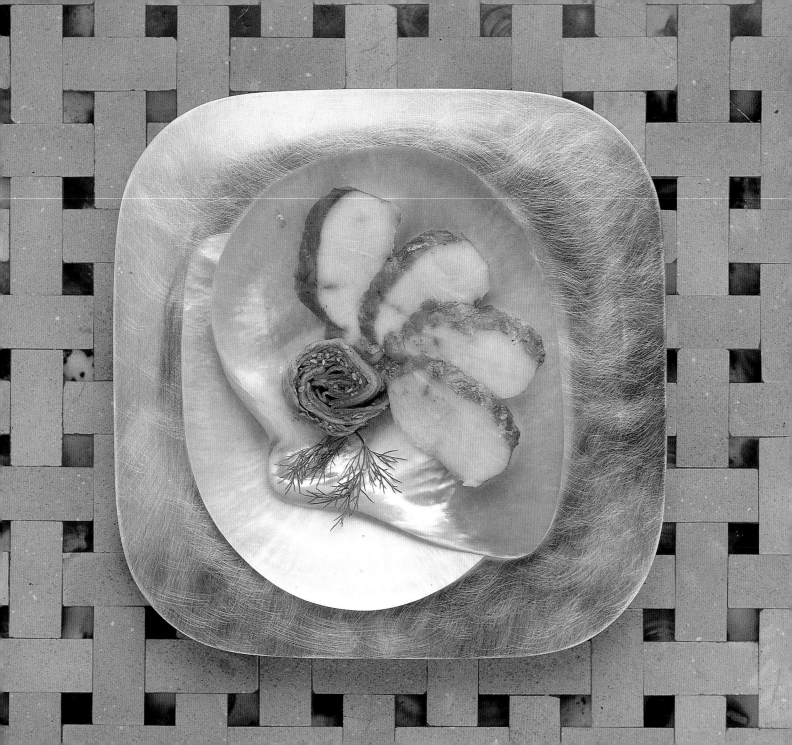

STUFFED DEEP-FRIED YAM DUMPLINGS

A Teochew delicacy filled with red-roasted pork (*char siew*). If *char siew* is not available at a Chinese store or market, make your own (page 41). ⏱⏱

1 yam, about 600 g (1¼ lb)
100 g (3½ oz) tapioca flour
100 g (3½ oz) pork oil (see Helpful hints), or vegetable shortening such as Crisco
1 tablespoon five-spice powder
1 teaspoon sesame oil
1 tablespoon sugar
½ teaspoon white pepper powder
oil for deep frying
1 teaspoon salt

Filling:
200 g (7 oz) red roasted pork (*char siew*), diced
50 g (1½ oz) frozen green peas, defrosted
1 small onion, finely diced
1 small carrot, diced
½ cup oyster sauce
½ teaspoon five-spice powder
½ teaspoon sesame oil
½ teaspoon sugar
2 tablespoons light soy sauce
1 tablespoon cornflour

Put all **filling** ingredients in a bowl and mix well. Set aside to chill in the refrigerator.

Peel yam and cut in pieces. Steam for about 30 minutes over boiling water until it is soft. Mash the yam and set aside. Mix the tapioca flour with boiling water and knead into a dough. Add the pork oil, five-spice powder, sesame oil, salt, sugar and pepper and the mashed yam. Mix thoroughly and divide into 10–12 portions. Flatten each portion into a round shape.

Divide the filling into 10–12 portions and put one in the middle of each piece of flattened yam dough. Squeeze together to enclose the filling and make into a dumpling. Heat oil in a wok or deep fryer and deep fry the yam dumplings until golden brown. Serve hot.

Helpful hints: Pork oil or lard is made by chopping hard (back) pork fat into fine dice and cooking over low heat with about 2 tablespoons water until the water evaporates and all the oil runs out.

ROJAK

Salad with Spicy Sauce

An unusual salad combining fruit and vegetables, drenched with a rather pungent sauce. The black shrimp paste, generally known as *hay koh* but sometimes referred to by its Indonesian name, *petis*, makes all the difference. ◑ ◐

- 1 yam bean, peeled and thickly sliced
- 1 green mango, peeled and thickly sliced
- 1 cucumber, sliced
- $^1/_4$ fresh pineapple, sliced
- 2 Chinese crullers, sliced (see Helpful hints)
- 4 dried beancurd, cut in cubes
- 20 stalks water convolvulus (*kangkung*), blanched in boiling water
- 2 cup beansprouts, blanched in boling water

Sauce:

- 500 g (1 lb) peanuts, deep fried and skin removed
- 5 cloves garlic, deep fried whole
- 1 teaspoon dried shrimp paste (*belacan*), grilled until fragrant
- 5 red chillies, seeds discarded
- 2 bird's-eye chillies
- 1 cup black shrimp paste (*hay koh*)
- 2 tablespoons tamarind, mixed with $^1/_2$ cup of water, squeezed and strained to obtain juice
- 2 teaspoons chopped palm sugar
- salt to taste

Make the **sauce** first. Pound or blend the peanuts, garlic, shrimp paste and chillies until fine. Add the black shrimp paste, tamarind water and palm sugar, mixing well to obtain a liquid paste. Season to taste with salt.

Prepare all the vegetables and arrange on a serving dish. Pour over 2 cups of sauce just before serving.

Helpful hints: Chinese crullers (C: *yu tiaow*) are two lengths of dough stuck together and deep fried. Sometimes called Chinese doughnuts, they are savoury rather than sweet and are traditionally eaten with rice porridge (congee).

MURTABAK

Savoury Stuffed Indian Bread

An Indian Muslim dish universally loved in Singapore, this is made from a feather-light dough filled with minced meat and fried on a griddle. Mutton would be the usual choice in Singapore, although lamb or even beef can be used. The texture is light and crisp, the filling wonderfully satisfying. This recipe makes 6 Murtabak, good as part of a lunch or a late-night snack. ☉ ☉

Dough:

   300 g (10 oz) plain flour
   100 ml (scant $^1/_2$ cup) fresh milk
   100 ml (scant $^1/_2$ cup) water
   1 whole egg, lightly beaten
   $^1/_2$ teaspoon sugar
   2 teaspoons butter
   $^1/_2$ teaspoon salt

Filling:

   2–3 tablespoons oil
   1 leek, finely sliced
   10 cloves garlic, finely chopped
   2 onions, finely chopped
   300 g (10 oz) minced lamb or beef
   6 eggs, lightly beaten

   about 3 tablespoons ghee or oil for frying

Make the **dough** first by kneading all ingredients except butter together to obtain a smooth dough. Cover and set aside in a warm place for 1 hour.

To prepare the **filling**, heat oil in the pan and sauté the garlic and onion until transparent and fragrant, then add the meat. Stir thoroughly and season to taste with salt and pepper. Set aside to cool, then mix together with the leek and egg.

Half an hour before the Murtabak are required, divide the dough into 6 equal portions and knead each portion with a little of the softened butter until smooth. Roll in balls and set aside for 30 minutes.

Roll each piece of dough as thinly as possible and cover with a cloth. Heat a heavy iron griddle or large frying pan until very hot and pour on a little ghee or oil. Place on a circle of dough, let it cook for about 1 minute, then spread the top with one-sixth of the filling. Fold in two sides of the dough, overlapping slightly. Repeat with the other two sides to make a package enclosing the filling. Cook until golden brown on one side, turn and cook on the other side. Repeat with the remaining dough and filling.

Serve the Murtabak hot with an accompaniment of plain sliced cucumber or sliced onion that has been salted for 1 hour, rinsed, squeezed dry and sprinkled with lime or lemon juice. A bowl of curry gravy can also be served for dipping the Murtabak.

TAUHU GORENG
Deep-fried Beancurd with Spicy Sauce

When sold as snack by hawkers or food stalls, fried beancurd is often cut in half diagonally and stuffed with a mixture of beansprouts and cucumber, with the sauce drizzled over. Served as part of a main meal, the beancurd can be sliced and arranged decoratively on a plate. 🕐🕐

2–3 cakes hard beancurd, deep fried until
    golden brown
100 g (3$\frac{1}{2}$ oz) beansprouts
1 small cucumber, finely shredded
2 spring onions, shredded

Sauce:
5 shallots, sliced
3 cloves garlic, sliced
5 red chillies, sliced
$\frac{1}{2}$ teaspoon dried shrimp paste (*belacan*)
1 tablespoon oil
200 g (7 oz) fried peanuts
3 tablespoons sweet black soy sauce
2 heaped tablespoons tamarind, soaked in
    $\frac{1}{2}$ cup water, squeezed and strained
    for juice

Prepare the **sauce** first. Fry the shallots, garlic, chillies and shrimp paste in oil until softened, then blend with peanuts. Add the soy sauce and tamarind juice to obtain a thick sauce.

Arrange the slices of fried beancurd on a plate and garnish with beansprouts, cucumber and spring onion. Pour over the sauce or serve separately if preferred.

Helpful hints: To save time, the sauce can be prepared well in advance. If sweet black sauce is not available, use regular black soy sauce sweetened with a little granulated white sugar.

YU SHENG

New Year Raw Fish Salad

This refreshing dish is found on the menu of just about every Singapore Chinese restaurant over the Lunar New Year period. It is considered auspicious as the term used for mixing the salad together sounds almost the same as the word symbolising good luck and prosperity. ① ① ①

Fish Mixture:

- 75 g (2$\frac{1}{2}$ oz) salmon fillet, thinly sliced (if not available, substitute with white fish fillet)
- 30 g (1 oz) white fish fillet, thinly sliced
- 1 tablespoon garlic oil (page 41)
- 5 cm (2 in) young ginger, finely shredded
- $\frac{1}{2}$ teaspoon white pepper powder
- 1 tablespoon fresh lime juice

Salad:

- 1 carrot, peeled and cut in matchsticks
- $\frac{1}{2}$ giant white radish, peeled and cut in matchsticks
- $\frac{1}{2}$ green radish, peeled and cut in matchsticks (if not available, use 1 whole giant white radish)
- 100 g (3$\frac{1}{2}$ oz) yam, peeled, cut in matchsticks and deep fried (half mixed with red and half with green food colouring)
- 60 g (2 oz) preserved sweet papaya or melon, sliced
- 50 g (1$\frac{1}{2}$ oz) sour leek, sliced
- 30 g (1 oz) preserved salted ginger, sliced
- 30 g (1 oz) preserved sweet red ginger, sliced
- 100 g (3$\frac{1}{2}$ oz) jellyfish, soaked and sliced
- 75 g (2$\frac{1}{2}$ oz) pomelo or grapefruit flesh, shredded by hand
- 4 fragrant lime leaves (*daun limau purut*), very finely sliced

Sauce:

- 4 tablespoons garlic oil (page 41)
- 1 teaspoon sesame oil
- 6 tablespoons Ribena or other blackcurrant syrup
- 2 tablespoons sour plum paste
- 1 tablespoon sour plum sauce

Garnish:

- 4 tablespoons fried peanuts, coarsely crushed
- $\frac{1}{2}$ tablespoon five-spice powder
- 1 tablespoon sesame seed, dry fried until golden
- flour crisps (page 41)

Prepare the ingredients for the **salad** and place on a large plate for presentation at the dinner table. Mix the **sauce** ingredients and set aside.

At serving time, mix the fish with garlic oil, ginger, pepper and lime juice. Pour the sauce over the top of the salad ingredients and sprinkle the **garnish** ingredients on top. The diners must all help mix the salad using a pair of chopsticks to ensure good luck.

SOTO AYAM

Spicy Chicken Soup with Noodles

As the ancestors of many Malay Singaporeans originally came from Java, it's not surprising that this Javanese noodle soup is found at most Singapore food centres. It's ideal as a light luncheon dish, or can be eaten as a starter to a main meal. ⊘⊘

1 large chicken, weighing about 1.5 kg (3 lb)
50 g (1½ oz) transparent noodles, soaked in hot water to soften
150 g (5 oz) beansprouts
5 hard-boiled eggs, peeled and quartered
5 tablespoons roughly chopped Chinese celery leaves
6 slices of Lontong (see Helpful hints), cut in large cubes (optional)
3 tablespoons fried shallots

Spice Paste:
15 shallots
10 cloves garlic
8 candlenuts
5 cm (2 in) ginger
6 cm (2½ in) fresh turmeric, or 2 teaspoons turmeric powder
2 tablespoons coriander powder
3 tablespoons oil
3 lemon grass, bruised
5 cm (2 in) galangal, sliced
8 fragrant lime leaves
salt and pepper to taste

Simmer the whole chicken in 6 cups water for 30 minutes.

To make the **spice paste**, chop the shallots, garlic, candlenuts, ginger and turmeric and put in a blender with just enough of the oil to keep the blades turning. Process until fine. Heat remaining oil in a heavy pan and sauté the blended paste together with remaining spice paste ingredients for 4–5 minutes, stirring frequently.

Put the cooked spice paste with the partially cooked chicken and simmer for another 20 minutes. Season soup to taste with salt and pepper. Remove the chicken from the stock, debone meat and cut into shreds. Strain stock and put back in the pan to reheat.

Divide the transparent noodles, hard-boiled eggs, beansprouts, celery leaves and chicken between 6 large bowls. Add some sliced Lontong if liked. Top with stock and sprinkle with fried shallots.

Helpful hints: Sliced Lontong (compressed rice roll) or deep-fried potato fritters are often added to make the Soto more substantial. Recipe for Lontong is on page 84.

KIAM CHYE TAUHU

Duck Soup with Salted Cabbage

One of the most popular soups in Singapore is made with either poultry or pork simmered with salted Chinese cabbage and melting soft beancurd. The use of duck as the main ingredient is generally reserved for festive occasions. ☻ ☻

1 fresh duck, weighing about 2 kg (5 lb)
3 tablespoons black soy sauce
1 tablespoon sesame oil
300 g (10 oz) salted Chinese cabbage, rinsed in fresh water
10 cm (4 in) young ginger, cut into 3 pieces and lightly bruised
1 piece dried Mandarin orange peel
1 cake soft beancurd, diced
salt and pepper to taste

Wash and dry the duck thoroughly and cut into two. Mix the soy sauce and sesame oil and rub all over the duck. Heat plenty of oil until very hot and deep fry the duck until golden brown. Remove and drain.

Boil 3 litres (12 cups) water to boil in a large pan. Add the duck, bring back to the boil and simmer for 30 minutes. Remove the duck from the stock.

Place the salted cabbage, ginger and dried orange peel into a bowl large enough to hold the duck. Add the duck, beancurd and enough stock to cover. Place the bowl in a steamer, cover and simmer over moderate heat for about 1 hour until the duck is tender. Season to taste with salt and a liberal amount of white pepper.

Helpful hints: 1 kg (2 lb) of pork ribs can be substituted for the duck if preferred, although the flavour is not as rich.

BAK KUT TEH

Spiced Pork Bone Soup

A popular hawker stall snack, eaten as a late-night or early morning pick-me-up or as a breakfast. It can be made using internal organs of the pig as well as bones and meat, although the version using ribs is most popular in Singapore today. Ⓔ Ⓔ

500 g (1 lb) pork ribs, cleaned and cut into 5 cm (2 in) lengths
250 g (8 oz) lean pork, in one piece
3 litres (12 cups) water

Seasoning:

4 *gan cao*
1 *luo han guo*
50 g (2½ oz) *dang xin*
25 g (1 oz) *chuan kong*
25 g (1 oz) *dang kway*
15 g (½ oz) *sheng di*
5 whole star anise
1 cinnamon stick, about 8 cm (3 in) long
10 cloves
1 piece dried Mandarin orange peel
½ cup light soy sauce
¼ cup black soy sauce
2 tablespoons sugar

Put the pork ribs and meat with water in a large pan. Wrap all the seasoning ingredients except soy sauces and sugar in a piece of clean cheesecloth and add the the pan. Add both lots of soy sauce, sugar and water and bring to the boil. Simmer gently, uncovered, for 1½ to 2 hours until the meat is almost falling off the bones. Season to taste with salt (if needed) and white pepper powder.

When serving, cut the lean pork meat into small pieces. Put in a bowl together with the pork ribs and top with the stock.

Helpful hints: The first six seasoning ingredients are Chinese herbs which should be available in any Chinese medicine shop. If they are not available, they can be omitted, although the flavour will be less rich and the soup presumably less of a restorative.

SOP KAMBING

Indian Mutton Soup

Also known as Sop Tulang or Bone Soup, this robust dish is one of the more popular stall foods in Singapore. It makes a great late-night supper or luncheon, especially if served with lots of crusty French bread. ⊙ ⊘

5 cm (2 in) ginger
6 cloves garlic
500 g (1 lb) meaty mutton or lamb ribs
1 heaped tablespoon coriander powder
1 teaspoon fennel powder
$\frac{1}{2}$ teaspoon cumin powder
2–3 litres (8–12 cups) water
2 tablespoons oil
2 leeks, sliced (white part only)
1 cinnamon stick 8 cm (3 in) long
4 whole star anise
5 cardamom pods, bruised
fried shallots to garnish
1 tomato, quartered
chopped Chinese celery or coriander leaves to
   garnish
1 teaspoon salt

Pound or blend the ginger and garlic together, then put in a pot with the mutton or lamb ribs, coriander, fennel, cumin and salt. Add 3 litres of water if using mutton, but only 2 litres if using lamb, which will cook more quickly. Simmer uncovered until the meat is soft.

Heat the oil in a small pan and sauté the leeks, shallots, cinnamon, star anise and cardamom until the leeks are tender. Add to the mutton soup and simmer for another couple of minutes. Add tomato, taste and add more salt if desired. Serve sprinkled with fried shallots and Chinese celery leaves, and accompany with crusty French bread.

HAE MEE
Prawn Noodle Soup

The flavour of this relatively simple noodle dish depends upon the richly flavoured stock, made from both fresh and dried prawns as well as pork or chicken. The soup is traditionally served with delicious crunchy little cubes of fried pork fat; a few Singaporeans now omit these for health reasons, but they make all the difference to the final flavour. ⓶ ⓵

> **8–12 large prawns**
> **100 g (3½ oz) hard back pork fat, cut in 0.5 cm (¼ in) dice (optional)**
> **150 g (5 oz) fresh egg noodles**
> **1 spring onion, finely sliced**
> **white pepper powder**

Stock:

> **1 tablespoon oil**
> **100 g (3½ oz) small fresh prawns**
> **3 tablespoons dried prawns**
> **1 dried chilli (optional)**
> **5 shallots, very finely chopped**
> **5 cloves garlic, very finely chopped**
> **5 whole white peppercorns, coarsely ground and gently fried until fragrant**
> **200 g (7 oz) pork or chicken bones**
> **2 litres (8 cups) water**
> **1 tablespoon sugar**

Peel the 8–12 large prawns, saving the head and shells for the stock but leaving the tails on. Put the prawns in the refrigerator.

To make the **stock**, heat the oil and fry the reserved prawn heads and shells together with the fresh small prawns, dried prawns and dried chilli. Cook over low heat, stirring, for about 5 minutes. Crush firmly with the back of a wooden spoon against the side of the pan, then add all other stock ingredients except the sugar. Simmer gently, uncovered, until the liquid is reduced by half.

Heat the sugar in a small pan with an equal amount of water and cook until it turns a dark caramel colour. Add to the stock. Sieve the stock, pressing firmly with the back of a spoon to extract all the liquid, then season to taste with salt. Keep hot if using immediately.

While the stock is cooking, put the pork dice in a pan (preferably non-stick) and cook gently until the oil runs out and the pork fat turns golden brown and crisp. Drain and set aside.

To finalise the dish, plunge the noodles in boiling water for about 1 minute to heat through, then divide between 4 bowls. Top with hot stock then add 2–3 prawns to each bowl. Sprinkle with the pork fat, spring onions and a liberal dash of white pepper. Serve immediately with sliced red chilli in a bowl of light soy sauce, or with the *sambal* of your choice.

Helpful hints: If liked, the stock can be made in bulk and deep frozen.

KWAY TEOW & VEGETARIAN BEEHOON

KWAY TEOW

Creamy fresh rice-flour noodles (*kway teow*) cooked with seafood make a delicious light lunch. ⏱

$\frac{1}{2}$ cup oil
1 teaspoon finely chopped garlic
2 eggs, lightly beaten
500 g (1 lb) fresh rice-flour noodles (*kway teow*)
2 tablespoons light soy sauce
4 tablespoons black soy sauce
1 cup chicken stock
75 g (2$\frac{1}{2}$ oz) red snapper fillet, sliced
10 medium-sized prawns, shelled
150 g (5 oz) squid, cleaned, skinned and sliced
2 pieces Chinese mustard greens (*chye sim*) cut in 3 cm (1$\frac{1}{4}$ in) lengths
75 g (2$\frac{1}{2}$ oz) beansprouts
$\frac{1}{2}$ teaspoons white pepper powder
1 teaspoon sesame oil
salt to taste

Heat oil in a wok and fry garlic for a few seconds. Add egg and cook until it starts to set. Add the noodles and stir well. Add the soy sauces and stock. Bring to the boil then add fish, prawns and squid. Cook over very high heat until the seafood is cooked, then add mustard greens, beansprouts, pepper and sesame oil. Stir fry over very high heat for another minute then serve.

VEGETARIAN BEEHOON

A simple light dish that can be eaten as a snack or as part of a main meal. ⏱

$\frac{1}{4}$ cup oil
8 cloves garlic, finely chopped
1 large onion, sliced
4 long white Chinese cabbage leaves, shredded
8 dried black Chinese mushrooms, soaked until soft then sliced
10–15 canned button mushrooms, sliced
1 carrot, cut in matchsticks
$\frac{1}{2}$ cup chicken stock
500 g (1 lb) dried rice vermicelli (*beehoon*), soaked in hot water to soften
4 tablespoons light soy sauce
8 tablespoons black soy sauce
1 heaped cup chopped Chinese mustard greens (*chye sim*), cut in 3 cm (1$\frac{1}{4}$ in) lengths
200 g (7 oz) beansprouts
salt and pepper to taste

Heat oil in a wok and fry the garlic for a few seconds. Add onion and cabbage, stir then add both lots of mushrooms and carrot. Pour in stock and stir fry over very high heat for half a minute. Add noodles, stir to mix well then put in both lots of soy sauce and salt and pepper to taste. Stir fry for 1 minute then add mustard greens and beansprouts. Cook until the greens have softened slightly then serve immediately.

Opposite:
Kway Teow (left) and Vegetarian Beehoon (right).

MEE SIAM

Rice Noodles in Spicy Soup

This Nonya speciality—noodles in a hot, sour gravy with the delightful tang of salted soya beans and tamarind—is a popular snack at food stalls throughout Singapore. Singaporean Indians have even developed their own version of Mee Siam and almost every Malay food stall also has its version. ① ①

150 g (5 oz) dried rice-flour vermicelli (*beehoon*), soaked in hot water to soften
100 g (3½ oz) beansprouts
2 cakes hard beancurd, fried and diced
5 dried deep-fried beancurd (*tau foo pok*), diced
2 hard-boiled eggs, shelled and cut in wedges, or 8 quail's eggs
spring onions or Chinese chives (*koo chye*) to garnish

Gravy:
30 dried chillies, cut and soaked to soften
6 cloves garlic
5 tablespoons dried prawns, soaked
1 teaspoon dried shrimp paste
5 tablespoons oil
½ cup fried peanuts, ground
½ cup salted soya beans (*tau cheo*), mashed
3 tablespoons sugar
3 tablespoons tamarind pulp, soaked in 1 cup water, squeezed and strained for juice
3 cups water
1 lemon grass, bruised

Prepare the sauce by blending the soaked chillies until ground into a paste. Measure 3 tablespoons of this and set aside. Pound or blend the garlic and dried prawns, adding a little of the oil if necessary to keep the blades turning.

Heat the oil and gently fry the blended paste and ground chilli for 2 minutes. Add the peanuts, salted soya beans and sugar and stir fry for another minute. Add the tamarind juice and water and bring to the boil. Simmer gently, uncovered, for about 5 minutes. Season to taste with salt and pepper.

Put 3 tablespoons of the sauce in a wok and stir fry the noodles for just long enough to mix well with the sauce and take on a red colour.

To serve, divide the soaked noodles between 4 bowls. Add the beansprouts, both lots of beancurd and egg. Pour on the gravy and serve garnished with spring onions or Chinese chives.

LAKSA LEMAK

Noodles in Spicy Coconut Gravy

Laksa is a meeting of Chinese and Malay styles of cooking, with a remarkably happy result: fresh rice-flour noodles bathed in spicy coconut milk, with chunks of seafood and deep-fried beancurd. A very satisfying snack or luncheon dish. ⏱

> 3 tablespoons oil
> 2 cups coconut milk
> 2 cups of chicken stock
> 100 g (3$\frac{1}{2}$ oz) prawns, shelled
> 100 g (3$\frac{1}{2}$ oz) squid, cleaned, skinned and sliced
> 6 fresh scallops (optional)
> 6 quail's eggs or 1 hen's egg, hard-boiled and peeled
> 6 dried deep-fried beancurd (*tau foo pok*)
> salt and pepper to taste
> 200 g (7 oz) fresh rice-flour noodles (*laksa*), blanched in boiling water, or dried rice vermicelli (*beehoon*), soaked to soften
> 1 cup beansprouts
> 2 sprigs *laksa* leaf, chopped roughly
> 2 tablespoons fried shallots

Spice Paste:

> 12 shallots
> 4 cloves garlic
> 6 candlenuts
> 5 cm (2 in) ginger
> 4 red chillies
> 2 tablespoons dried prawns, soaked to soften
> 2 tablespoons fish curry powder
> 1 teaspoon dried shrimp paste (*belacan*)
> 2 lemon grass, bruised

Prepare the **spice paste** first. Chop the shallots, garlic, candlenuts, ginger and chillies coarsely and blend or process with the dried prawns and a little of the oil until fine. Mix in the curry powder and dried shrimp paste, blend for a few seconds longer, then set aside with the lemon grass.

Heat the remaining oil in a wok or heavy pan. Add the spice paste and cook over low heat, stirring constantly, for about 5 minutes until the paste is fragrant. Add coconut milk and chicken stock and bring to the boil, stirring. Put in all the seafood and the beancurd and simmer until cooked. Season to taste.

To serve, divide the noodles and beansprouts between 4–6 bowls. Top with the coconut milk sauce and sprinkle with *laksa* leaf and fried shallots.

Helpful hints: The coconut-milk gravy can be prepared several hours in advance and re-heated just before serving. Although *laksa* leaf adds a distinctive touch, omit if not available as nothing else tastes remotely like this pungent herb.

HOKKIEN FRIED NOODLES

As the majority of Singapore's Chinese population is Hokkien, this is the all-time favourite noodle dish. Fresh egg noodles are stir fried with fresh or dried rice-flour noodles, a mixture of seafood, vegetable and pork, the whole lot bathed in rich stock and seasoned to perfection. Robust rather than refined, it makes an excellent lunch or late-night supper. The following recipe serves two; double for serving 3–4 people. ◐ ◑

$\frac{1}{3}$ cup oil
1 heaped teaspoon finely chopped garlic
30 g (1$\frac{1}{2}$ oz) red snapper fillet, cut in slices
75 g (2$\frac{1}{2}$ oz) medium prawns, shelled
1 small squid, cleaned and sliced
75 g (2$\frac{1}{2}$ oz) sliced pork
150 g (5 oz) fresh yellow noodles
50 g (1$\frac{1}{2}$ oz) dried rice vermicelli (*beehoon*)
2–3 leaves Chinese mustard greens (*chye sim*), cut in 3 cm (1$\frac{1}{4}$ in) lengths
2 leaves Chinese long white cabbage, sliced
2 tablespoons light soy sauce
$\frac{1}{2}$ teaspoon white pepper powder
1 teaspoon sesame oil
1 egg, lightly beaten
fresh coriander and finely shredded carrot to garnish

Stock:
1 kg (2 lb) chicken bones
1 kg (2 lb) pork bones
8 cm (3 in) ginger, bruised
3 cloves garlic, bruised
1$\frac{1}{2}$ litres (6 cups) water

Prepare the **stock** first. Blanch both lots of bones in boiling water for 3 minutes. Discard water and bring 1$\frac{1}{2}$ litres water to the boil with the bones, ginger and garlic. Simmer uncovered over very low heat for 2 hours. Drain and set stock aside.

When noodles are required, heat oil in a wok then add the garlic and sauté for a few seconds. Add the fish, prawns, squid and pork. Stir fry over high heat for a minute then pour in 1$\frac{1}{2}$–2 cups stock (see Helpful hints) and simmer for another minute. Add both lots of noodles, vegetables, soy sauce, pepper and sesame oil. Stir thoroughly until all ingredients are mixed, then add the egg and cook for a few seconds until set. Serve with Sambal Belacan (page 39) and halved small round limes (*limau kesturi*).

Helpful hints: It is essential to cook the noodles over very high heat to ensure that the stock evaporates to a small amount of rich liquid by the time the noodles are cooked. If your cooker cannot achieve very high temperatures, reduce the stock when boiling to just 1$\frac{1}{2}$ cups and add this, rather than 2 cups of stock, when cooking the noodles.

CLAYPOT RICE

A simple Cantonese one-pot dish, where rice is cooked with chicken, fragrant Chinese sausage, mushrooms and seasonings. The Chinese believe that a claypot is essential to ensure the correct flavour and fragrance of this dish, though any other type of covered earthenware container could be used. ⏱

2 cups long-grain rice, washed
3 cups chicken stock
$^1/_2$ fresh chicken, about 750 g (1$^1/_2$ lb),
    cut into small cubes
1 Chinese sausage, sliced
6 dried black mushrooms, soaked, simmered
    until cooked and quartered
4 cm (1$^1/_2$ in) ginger, thinly sliced
1 spring onion, thinly sliced

Marinade:

2 tablespoons oil
3 tablespoons oyster sauce
1 tablespoon soya sauce
1 tablespoon Chinese wine
$^1/_2$ teaspoon sesame oil
1 teaspoon black soy sauce
1 teaspoon sugar
$^1/_2$ teaspoon white pepper powder
1 tablespoon cornflour

Put the rice in a claypot with chicken stock, cover and cook over low heat for about 20 minutes.

While the rice is cooking, mix the **marinade** ingredients together and pour over the chicken, mixing well. When the rice has cooked for 20 minutes, spread the marinated chicken, Chinese sausage, mushrooms and sliced ginger on top. Cover and cook for another 10 minutes. Sprinkle with spring onions and serve.

AUBERGINE MASALA & POTATO CURRY

AUBERGINE MASALA ☺☺

500 g (1 lb) long slender aubergine (*brinjal*)
$^1/_4$ cup oil
1 large onion, thinly sliced
3 cloves garlic, thinly sliced
$^1/_2$ teaspsoon fenugreek
1 teaspoon cumin seeds
2 tablespoons tamarind, soaked in $^1/_4$ cup
   warm water, squeezed and strained to
   obtain juice
1 cup plain yoghurt
salt to taste

Marinade:

2 teaspoons coriander powder
1–2 teaspoons chilli powder
1 teaspon cumin powder
$^1/_2$ teaspoon turmeric powder

Opposite:
Potato Curry (left)
and Aubergine
Masala (right)

Cut the aubergine in lengthwise slices 1 cm ($^1/_2$ in) thick. Combine the **marinade**, sprinkle over the aubergine and set aside for 15 minutes.

Heat the oil in a wok or heavy saucepan and gently fry the onion and garlic until golden. Add the fenugreek and cumin seeds and continue cooking for another minute before adding the spiced aubergine. Mix well, season with salt and add tamarind juice. Cook, stirring from time to time, until the aubergine is tender. Add the yoghurt and reheat gently. Remove from heat and serve.

POTATO CURRY ☺☺

5 cloves garlic
3 cm ($1^1/_4$ in) ginger
3 tablespoons oil
1 large onion, sliced
2 tablespoons coriander powder
1 tablespoon chilli powder
1 teaspoon turmeric powder
1 teaspoon cumin powder
2 cloves
1 cinnamon stick, about 4 cm ($1^1/_2$ in) long
10 curry leaves
500 g (1 lb) potatoes, cut into pieces
2 teaspoons freshly squeezed lime or lemon
   juice
2 tomatoes, cut into wedges
6 stalks coriander leaves, chopped
salt and pepper to taste
1 cup yoghurt

Blend garlic and ginger together. Heat oil and sauté onion until golden. Add the garlic-ginger paste, all the spices and the curry leaves. Continue cooking over low heat, stirring frequently for 4–5 minutes. Add the potatoes and sauté until they are well coated with spices. Put in 2 cups water and simmer until the potatoes are cooked. Add lemon juice, tomato wedges and coriander leaves. Season to taste with salt and pepper. Add yoghurt and heat gently before serving.

SPICY KANGKUNG & FRIED BEANSPROUTS

SPICY KANGKUNG

A favourite way of cooking this excellent leafy green vegetable, using both Malay and Chinese seasonings. ☉

1 kg (2 lb) water convolvulus (*kangkung*)
3 tablespoons dried shrimps, soaked to soften
6 cloves garlic
6 shallots
5 red chillies
2.5 cm (1 in) ginger
2 teaspoons dried shrimp paste (*belacan*)
3–4 tablespoons oil
2 tablespoons sugar
1 teaspoon sesame oil
1 tablespoon light soy sauce
salt and pepper to taste
1 red chilli, finely sliced

Opposite:
Beansprouts with
Salted Fish (left)
and Spicy
Kangkung (right)

Use tender tips and leaves of the *kangkung*, discarding tough stems. Pound or blend the dried shrimps until fine. Set aside. Blend garlic, shallots, chillies and ginger until fine, using a little of the oil if necessary to keep the blades turning. Add the shrimp paste and blend for another few seconds.

Heat the remaining oil in the wok or heavy pan and add the blended mixture together with the dried shrimps. Cook over low heat, stirring frequently, for about 5 minutes until fragrant. Add sugar, sesame oil and soy sauce, stirring until well mixed, then add

kangkung and stir well. Cook with the lid on until the *kangkung* is tender. Season to taste with salt and pepper and sprinkle with sliced chilli.

BEANSPROUTS WITH SALTED FISH ☉

100 g (3½ oz) salted fish, finely sliced
2 tablespoons cornflour
oil for deep frying
2 tablespoons oil
½ large onion, finely chopped
2.5 cm (1 in) ginger, finely sliced
3 dried black mushrooms, soaked and sliced
500 g (1 lb) beansprouts
2 spring onions, cut in 2.5 cm (1 in) lengths
4 coarse chive plants (*koo chye*), cut in 2.5 cm (1 in) lengths
4 tablespoons oyster sauce
½ teaspoon sesame oil
1 tablespoon Chinese wine
salt and pepper to taste

Put the fish and cornflour in a plastic bag and shake a few times to coat fish. Shake then deep fry in oil over moderate heat until crisp and golden brown.

Heat 2 tablespoons fresh oil. Cook onions, ginger and mushrooms for a minute over moderate heat, then add all other ingredients. Increase heat to maximum and stir fry until the beansprouts are just cooked. Serve scattered with the salted fish.

STUFFED BEANCURD IN CRABMEAT SAUCE

In recent years, fine-textured Japanese "silken" beancurd has become very popular in Singapore. It is shaped into a roll and packed in a plastic tube about 15–20 cm (6–8 in) in length. This dish would be served as part of a main meal together with rice, accompanied, for example, by a leafy green vegetable and another one or two poultry, meat or fish dishes, plus a soup. ⊘⊘

3 tubes Japanese "silken" beancurd

Stuffing:
100 g (3¹/₂ oz) white fish fillet
100 g (3¹/₂ oz) peeled prawns
1 spring onion, finely sliced
1 tablespoon cornflour
1 egg white
salt and pepper to taste
1 spring onion, finely sliced
egg yolk to garnish (optional)

Sauce:
60 g (2 oz) crabmeat
1 cup chicken stock
¹/₂ teaspoon sesame oil
¹/₂ teaspoon sugar
1 tablespoon Chinese wine
salt and pepper to taste
1 tablespoon cornflour mixed with 2 tablespoons water

Prepare the **stuffing** first by blending the fish and prawn meat together until fine. Add the remaining ingredients and blend just to mix well.

Use a very sharp knife to cut the plastic tubes of beancurd across the middle and gently squeeze out the beancurd rolls. Cut each piece into 2.5 cm (1 in) slices. Use a teaspoon to scoop out a small hollow in the centre of each slice and fill with a little of the stuffing. Place on a plate inside a steamer and steam for 5 minutes.

While the beancurd is steaming, prepare the **sauce**. Put the chicken stock, crabmeat, sesame oil and sugar in a saucepan and bring to the boil. Add Chinese wine, season to taste with salt and pepper and thicken with cornflour. When serving, pour the sauce over the beancurd and sprinkle with spring onion. Garnish the top of each beancurd slice with a little crumbled egg yolk if liked.

Helpful hints: Japanese beancurd is often sold in supermarkets and in Asian speciality stores abroad. It is very delicate, so be careful when handling it.

SAYUR LEMAK WITH LONTONG

Vegetables in Coconut Milk with Compressed Rice

This seasoned vegetable stew with compressed rice (Lontong) can be served as part of a main meal or eaten alone for breakfast or lunch. ☺☺☺

3 cakes hard beancurd, halved and deep fried
2 cups coconut milk
salt and pepper to taste

Seasoning:

3 tablespoons dried prawns, soaked
20 shallots
10 cloves garlic
10–15 red chillies
2.5 cm (1 in) fresh turmeric, or 1 teaspoon turmeric powder
1 tablespoon coriander powder
2.5 cm (1 in) galangal, sliced
2 tablespoons oil
1 teaspoon dried shrimp paste (*belacan*)

Vegetables:

1 small slender aubergine, sliced crosswise
1 carrot, peeled and sliced
8 leaves long white Chinese cabagge, cut into bite-size chunks
20 long beans, cut in 5 cm (2 in) lengths

Lontong:

½ cup long-grain rice, washed
2 pieces banana leaf about 35 x 30 cm (14 x 12 in), or 2 self-sealing plastic bags

Prepare the **lontong** first. If banana leaf is available, place one square on top of the other and roll into a cylinder about 6 cm (2½ in) in diameter. Seal the lower end using a toothpick. Put the rice into the roll; it should come one-third of the way up. Fold over and secure the top end of the roll, leaving the two-thirds empty for the rice to fill as it expands during cooking. Put in a pan of boiling water, cover and simmer very slowly for 2–2½ hours. Let cool to room temperature before serving.

If banana leaf is not available, use two zip-lock (self-sealing) plastic bags three times the size of the amount of rice. Put the rice in one bag and seal. Place this inside the second bag and seal. Pierce through both bags to allow the water to penetrate. Cook as described above.

While the Lontong is cooking, prepare the **seasoning**. Pound or blend the dried prawns, shallots, garlic, chillies and turmeric until fine. Mix with the coriander and galangal. Heat the remaining oil and stir fry the dried shrimp paste until fragrant. Add the blended paste and fry for 5 minutes.

Bring 4 cups of water to the boil and simmer the **vegetables** until half-cooked. Add the fried seasoning and simmer until vegetables are tender. Put in the beancurd and chillies, simmer a minute longer, then add the coconut milk. Stir until well heated then season to taste with chunks of Lontong.

IKAN PARI PANGGANG
Barbecued Stingray

Stingray was an inexpensive and largely ignored fish until relatively recently, when this excellent way of cooking it—slathered with chilli sambal, wrapped in banana leaf and grilled over charcoal—filtered down from neighbouring Malaysia. Needless to say, the price of stingray has risen with the popularity of this dish. If you can't obtain stingray, try using any white fish fillets. �---

600 g (1¹/₄ lb) stingray wings, or white fish fillets
salt and pepper to taste
2 tablespoons juice from small round limes (*limau kesturi*) or regular lime or lemon juice
1 large piece banana leaf (about 30 cm/12 in square), or baking paper and aluminium foil
¹/₂ cup Chilli Sambal (page 38)

Wash the stingray and season with salt, white pepper and lime juice. Place in banana leaf and cover both sides of the stingray with Chilli Sambal. Fold in the banana leaf to make a package and cook over a low charcoal fire for about 5 minutes; turn and grill the other side.

Place the banana leaf package on a large plate, unwrapping it at the table to serve.

Helpful hints: Banana leaf gives a special flavour and texture during cooking as it releases its moisture into the enclosed food. Wrapping food inside waxed or any baking paper before putting it inside aluminium foil is an alternative, although something will be lacking from the final flavour.

ACAR IKAN

Braised Fish in Pickled Vegetables

A traditional Malay/Indonesian dish which can be found in many food stalls and coffee shops, this piquant way of cooking fish gets its name because it includes the seasonings and vinegar typically used for Acar (Pickled Vegetables). ⏱⏱

1 whole red snapper or bream, about
    750 g (1½ lb), or 500 g (1 lb) fish fillets
2 cloves garlic
3 tablespoons lime juice
salt and pepper to taste
oil for deep frying

Sauce:

10 shallots
8 cloves garlic
10 candlenuts
5 cm (2 in) ginger
5 cm (2 in) turmeric
2 tablespoons oil
2 lemon grass, bruised
10 whole shallots
15 bird's-eye chillies
100 g (3½ oz) cucumber, skin left on and cut
    in 0.5 cm (¼ in) wide strips, 5 cm (2 in)
    long
1 tablespoon sugar
¼ cup white vinegar
1 cup water
salt and pepper to taste

Clean the fish well inside and out, leaving on the head if liked. Pound the garlic and mix with lime juice, salt and pepper. Cut two deep diagonal slashes on both sides of the fish and rub it with the pounded mixture. Leave to marinate for 10 minutes, then deep fry in hot oil until golden brown and half-cooked.

While the fish is frying, prepare the **sauce**. Cut, then pound or blend the shallots, garlic, candlenuts, ginger and turmeric until fine, adding a little oil if necessary to keep the blades turning. Heat remaining oil in the heavy pan and stir fry the blended ingredients for about 5 minutes until fragrant. Add all the remaining sauce ingredients. Simmer for 3 minutes and season to taste with salt and pepper. Add more vinegar if a sour taste is preferred.

When the fish is golden brown, transfer to the pan with the sauce and simmer over low heat for about 5 minutes. Turn the fish carefully and cook for another 3–5 minutes, until the fish is cooked. Serve with white rice.

SOTONG & IKAN SAMBAL BELACAN
Deep-fried Squid & Fish with Spicy Sauce

DEEP-FRIED SQUID ②②

1 kg (2 lb) baby squid, 4–5 cm (1–1$\frac{1}{2}$ in) long
oil for deep frying

Marinade:

    3 tablespoons fish curry powder
    2 tablespoons light soy sauce
    1 tablespoon sugar
    1 teaspoon sesame oil
    3 tablespoons cornflour
    1 egg, lightly beaten

Sauce:

    2 tablespoons oil
    4 tablespoons honey
    2 tablespoons tomato sauce
    1 tablespoon each Lea & Perrins sauce, fresh
       lime juice, chilli sauce and light soy sauce
    1 teaspoon sesame oil
    1 teaspoon black soy sauce
    1 cup chicken stock
    2 tablespoons cornflour mixed with 4 table-
       spoons water

Wash and dry the squid thoroughly, but do not remove tentacles or skin. Mix all the **marinade** ingredients and combine with cleaned squid and leave to marinate while preparing sauce.

To make the **sauce**, heat the oil in a wok or heavy saucepan then add all the ingredients except blended cornflour. Bring to the boil then add corn-flour and cook over low heat, stirring, until the sauce thickens and clears. Heat oil in a wok until very hot. Fry the marinated squid until crisp and brown, then drain. Stir into the sauce and serve immediately.

FISH WITH SPICY SAUCE ②

1 sole or any other flat white fish, about 600–
    750 g (1$\frac{1}{4}$–1$\frac{1}{2}$ lb), or fish fillets
1 heaped tablespoon dried shrimps, soaked
4 cloves garlic
4 shallots
4 red chillies, seeded
2 tablespoons dried shrimp paste (*belacan*),
    toasted
1 lemon grass, cut into 2.5 cm (1 in) slices
1 tablespoon sugar
4 tablespoons light soy sauce
1 tablespoon sesame oil

Clean the fish thoroughly inside and out and season with salt and white pepper. Set aside.

Blend dried shrimps, garlic, shallots, chillies and shrimp paste. Heat oil and fry the blended ingredients, lemon grass and sugar. Cook over low heat, stirring frequently, for about 5 minutes. Add the soy sauce and sesame oil. Heat plenty of oil in a wok and deep fry the fish until cooked and golden brown. Drain fish and serve topped with the sauce.

MACCHI TANDOORI & RAITA

Marinated Baked Fish & Cucumber in Yoghurt Dressing

MACCHI TANDOORI

Tandoori chicken, marinated in a special blend of spices and roasted in a special clay oven or *tandoor*, is a northern Indian classic very popular in Singapore. This version uses fish, which goes well with Cucumber Raita. ◔ ◔

750 g (1½ lb) white fish fillets
1 lime or lemon, cut in wedges

Tandoori paste:
2.5 cm (1 in) fresh turmeric, or 1 teaspoon turmeric powder
25 shallots
4 cm (1½ in) ginger
10 cloves garlic
2 tablespoons chilli powder
1 tablespoon Tandoori powder
1 teaspoon salt
¼ teaspoon white pepper powder
1 cup yoghurt
1 tablespoon lemon juice

Make the **Tandoori paste** by pounding or blending the turmeric, shallots, ginger and garlic together until fine, adding a little of the yoghurt if necessary to keep the blades turning. Mix this with the remaining paste ingredients.

Rub both sides of each fish fillet with this mixture and leave to marinate for at least 1 hour.

Place fish on a rack set inside a baking dish and cook in a hot oven (200°C/400°F) for 15–20 minutes. Serve hot with wedges of lime, accompanied by Cucumber Raita.

CUCUMBER RAITA

Raitas, soothing yoghurt-based side dishes, are an excellent foil to any spicy Indian food. Although they are made with a wide variety of vegetables and even bananas, Cucumber Raita is perhaps the most popular. ◔

2 cucumbers, peeled
1 tablespoon salt
2 cups plain yoghurt
20 mint leaves, roughly chopped

Halve the cucumbers lengthwise and remove the seeds. Cut in thin slices and put in a bowl sprinkled with salt. Leave to marinate for about 10 minutes, then squeeze out the water. Rinse and drain.

Mix the cucumber slices with yohurt and mint leaves. Taste and add salt if desired. Can be sprinkled with a little freshly ground chilli or cumin powder if liked.

CHILLI CRAB & BLACK PEPPER CRAYFISH

CHILLI CRAB

This is virtually Singapore's national dish. ⏰⏰

1 kg (2 lb) fresh crabs, cleaned and halved
oil for deep frying
4 cloves garlic, finely chopped
5 cm (2 in) young ginger, roughly chopped
3 red chillies, finely chopped
$\frac{1}{4}$ cup chilli sauce
$\frac{1}{4}$ cup tomato sauce
1 teaspoon sesame oil
1 tablespoon sugar
1 tablespoon light soy sauce
1 cup chicken stock
1 tablespoon cornflour, mixed with 3 table-
    spoons water
1 egg, lightly beaten
salt and pepper to taste
1 spring onion, sliced

Opposite:
Black Pepper
Crayfish (left) and
Chilli Crab (right)

Deep fry the crabs in hot oil just until bright red. Remove and set aside. Pour out the oil and put $\frac{1}{4}$ cup fresh oil into the wok. Heat and add garlic, ginger and chilli. Stir until fragrant then add chilli sauce, tomato sauce, sugar, soy sauce and sesame oil. Simmer for 1 minute then season to taste with salt and pepper. Add the fried crab and stir to coat well with sauce. Put in the chicken stock and cook over high heat for 3 minutes. Stir thoroughly and thicken with cornflour and egg. Season to taste with salt and pepper and sprinkle with spring onions.

BLACK PEPPER CRAYFISH ⏰⏰

2 kg (5 lb) crayfish (flathead or slipper
    lobsters), halved lengthwise
oil for deep frying

Sauce:
100 g ($3\frac{1}{2}$ oz) butter
7 red chilli, seeded and very finely chopped
7 cloves garlic, finely chopped
2.5 cm (1 in) ginger, very finely chopped
2 tablespoons oyster sauce
2 tablespoons light soy sauce
2 teaspoons black soy sauce
1 tablespoon sugar
3 tablespoons black pepper, crushed

Heat oil until very hot then deep fry the crayfish until the shell changes colour. Set aside. Melt the butter in a wok or pan, add chilli, garlic and ginger and fry, stirring frequently, for about 3 minutes.

Add oyster sauce, both lots of soy sauce and sugar. Simmer over low heat for 30 seconds then add the black pepper. Continue cooking until the sauce thickens, then add the crayfish. Keep stirring until the crayfish is well coated with sauce, and cook for another couple of minutes. Serve hot.

Helpful hints: Prawns or crabs can be substituted for the crayfish if preferred.

FISH-HEAD CURRY

This dish was created back in the 1950s by a cook who came to Singapore from the southwest Indian state of Kerala, where this dish is unheard of. Its popularity spread and now there are dozens of different versions of fish-head curry. ✆✆

1 large fresh red snapper fish head, 750 g–1 kg (1¹/₂–2 lb)
5 small okra (ladies' fingers), halved
1 long slender aubergine, cut into 6 pieces
1 tomato, quartered
2 heaped tablespoons tamarind pulp, soaked in water and strained for juice

Sauce:
10 cloves garlic
20 shallots
10 red chillies
5 cm (2 in) ginger
2.5 cm (1 in) turmeric
1 lemon grass
20 curry leaves
¹/₄ cup oil
3 tablespoons fish curry powder
2 cups water
2 cups coconut milk
1 teaspoon salt
1 tablespoon sugar

Blanch the fish head in boiling water for about 3 minutes, then put it in iced water.

To prepare the **sauce,** chop coarsely then pound or blend the garlic, shallots, chillies, ginger, turmeric and lemon grass until fine, adding a little of the oil if necessary to keep the blades turning. Heat the remaining oil in a large pan and fry the blended mixture and curry leaves over low heat, stirring frequently, until fragrant (about 5 minutes). Add the curry powder and continue cooking for another couple of minutes.

Add 1 cup of water and simmer for a couple of minutes. Add remaining water, coconut milk, salt and the fish head. Bring to the boil over low heat then simmer, uncovered, until the fish is almost cooked. Add the okra and aubergine and simmer until cooked. Season to taste with salt and sugar, then add the tomato wedges just before serving.

Helpful hints: If you've never eaten fish head before, you might be a little cautious about trying it. Be reassured that it adds a special sweetness and texture to the curry, and the fish flesh (especially from the small cheek pockets) is delicious.

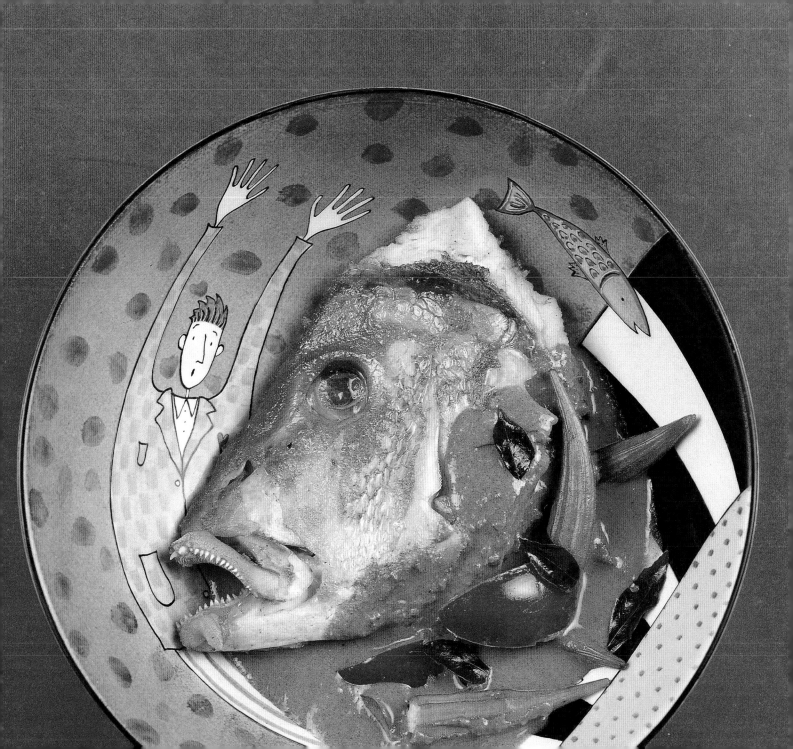

TEOCHEW FISH & OYSTER OMELETTE

TEOCHEW STEAMED FISH ◷

1 whole pomfret, about 1 kg (2 lb)
50 g (1½ oz) salted Chinese cabbage (*kiam chye*), chopped
1 tomato, cut in wedges
8 cm (3 in) ginger, finely sliced
2 red chillies, sliced
6 salted plums (obtainable in jars)
1 spring onion, cut in 5 cm (2 in) lengths
3 dried black mushrooms, soaked to soften then sliced
60 g (2 oz) shredded pork (optional)

Seasoning:

4 tablespoons garlic oil (page 41)
4 tablespoons oyster sauce
1 teaspoon sesame oil
2 tablespoons light soy sauce
1 tablespoon sugar
2 tablespoons Chinese wine
2 tablespoons cornflour, mixed with 4 table-spoons water
½ cup chicken stock

Opposite:
Teochew Steamed Fish (left) and Oyster Omelette (right)

Clean and dry the pomfret thoroughly. Combine all other ingredients except seasonings in a bowl.

Combine all seasoning ingredients and mix well. Stir into the bowl with the other items and mix. Lay the pomfret on a plate which will fit into a steamer or on a tray inside a wok and spread the mixture on top of the pomfret. Cover and steam over rapidly boiling water for 15–20 minutes until the fish is cooked. Do not overcook or the texture will be spoiled.

OYSTER OMELETTE ◷

8–10 large fresh oysters
2 tablespoons tapioca flour
1 tablespoon rice flour
8 tablespoons water
1 tablespoon oil
2 cloves garlic, finely chopped
3 whole eggs, beaten
1 tablespoon light soy sauce
1 tablespoon Chinese wine
white pepper powder
sprigs of fresh coriander to garnish

Wash the oysters and drain well. Mix both lots of flour together with the water to make a very thin batter. Heat a large heavy frying pan until very hot and add oil. Pour in the batter and cook for about 15 seconds before adding the beaten egg.

When the eggs are almost set, make a hole in the centre, pour in a little oil and fry the garlic for a few second. Mix then season with soy sauce, Chinese wine and pepper. Add oysters and cook just long enough to heat through. Serve sprinkled with fresh coriander and accompanied by a chilli sambal.

UDANG HALIA & UDANG ASAM

Prawns with Ginger & Sour Spicy Prawns

UDANG HALIA ⏱⏱

1 kg (2 lb) large fresh prawns
2 tablespoons oil
2.5 cm (1 in) ginger, very finely shredded

Sauce:

   8 red chillies – start w 4
   15 shallots
   10 cloves garlic
   8 cm (3 in) ginger
   5 cm (2 in) fresh turmeric, or 1 teaspoon
     turmeric powder
   3 lemon grass, bruised
   5 fragrant lime leaves (*daun limau purut*)
   1 cup water
   2 cups coconut milk
   salt and pepper to taste

Remove the heads and shells from the prawns and keep; leave on the tails. To prepare the **sauce**, chop then pound or blend the chillies, shallots, garlic, ginger and turmeric, adding a little of the oil if necessary to keep the blades turning. Heat the remaining oil in a saucepan and stir fry the blended ingredients together with the prawn shells and heads, lemon grass and lime leaves.

When the prawn shells have turned pink, add the water and simmer for 5 minutes. Add coconut milk and bring to the boil. Simmer uncovered over low heat for about 10 minutes, then season to taste with salt and pepper. Sieve the sauce then put back into the pan, adding prawns and finely shredded ginger. Simmer until the prawns are tender.

UDANG ASAM ⏱⏱

1 kg (2 lb) fresh large prawns
3 tablespoons lime juice
salt and pepper to taste
oil for deep frying

Sauce:

   3 shallots
   5 cloves garlic
   2 cm (3/4 in) galangal
   5 red chillies, finely sliced
   5 tablespoons palm sugar syrup or honey
   4 heaped tablespoons tamarind pulp, soaked in
     1 cup water, squeezed and strained

Peel the prawns, discarding the head but leaving on the tail. Pat dry, then deep fry the prawns. Blend the first 3 **sauce** ingredients, using a little oil if necessary. Heat 1 tablespoon oil and sauté the blended ingredients for about 5 minutes. Add remaining sauce ingredients and simmer until thick. Process in a blender for a few seconds then strain. Add prawns and stir until well coated with the sauce.

Opposite:
Udang Asam (top) and Udang Halia (below left)

STEAMED SEABASS WITH SAUCE

Creative Singapore cooks have never hesitated when it comes to borrowing new ingredients. English fruity chutney sauces, Worcestershire sauce and tomato sauce were incorporated into Chinese dishes decades ago. The latest new ingredient is Italian balsamic vinegar, which is blended with soy sauce and sesame oil to make this delightful dish ideal for a light luncheon. 🕐 🕐

1 seabass fillet, about 400 g (13 oz)
salt and pepper
5 baby kale (*kai lan*), blanched briefly in
    boiling water
1 clove garlic, finely chopped
2 teaspoons oil
1 tablespoon light soy sauce
1 teaspoon sesame oil
1 tablespoon balsamic vinegar
1 tablespoon garlic flakes (page 41)

Sprinkle the fish lightly on both sides with salt and pepper. Put on a plate and steam for 10 minutes.

While the fish is steaming, sauté the chopped garlic in oil for a few seconds then add the kale and stir-fry until cooked. Set aside.

Combine soy sauce, sesame oil and vinegar in a small saucepan and heat. Set aside. When the seabass is cooked, pour the sauce on top, sprinkle with garlic flakes and garnish with sauteed baby kale.

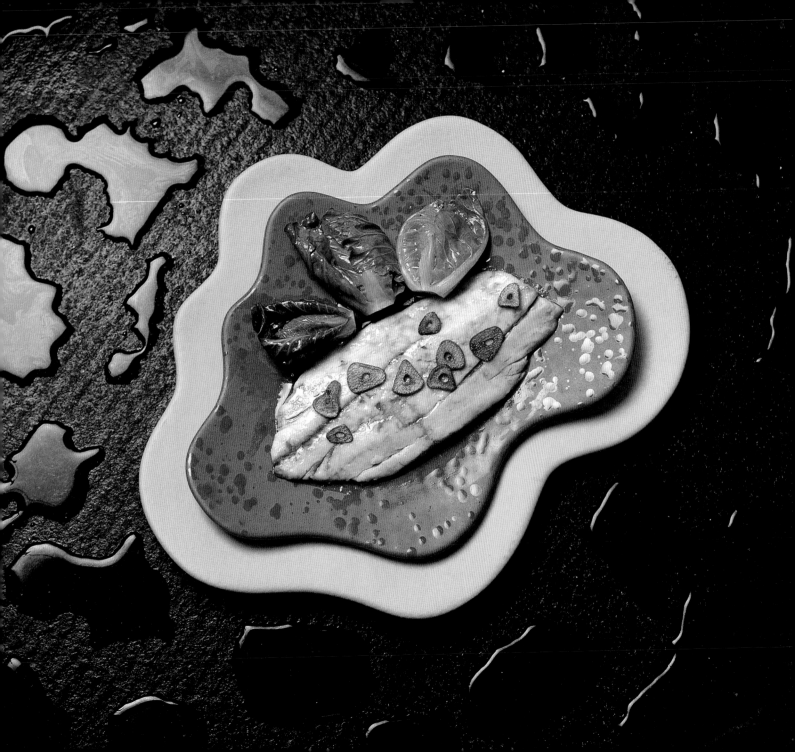

CRISPY CHICKEN WITH PRAWN MEAT

Every Cantonese restaurant offers crispy skin chicken, prepared by drenching the bird with a seasoned liquid and drying it thoroughly before deep frying in very hot oil. This dish, a variation on that theme, is not too complex to prepare at home for a special occasion. Both the chicken and the seasoned prawn stuffing can be prepared in advance, leaving the final assembly and frying to the last minute. ⊘⊘

1 large chicken weighing about 2 kg (4 lb)
2 litres (8 cups) water
1 cup Chinese red vinegar
1 cup Chinese wine
2 large limes or lemons, sliced
3 tablespoons glucose syrup or corn syrup

Stuffing:
500 g (1 lb) peeled prawns
1 spring onion, finely sliced
6 stalks fresh coriander, finely chopped
1 teaspoon salt
$\frac{1}{2}$ teaspoon sugar
1 tablespoon cornflour
1 egg white

Using a cleaver or strong knife, cut the chicken along the backbone. Remove the backbone and ribcage, leaving in the leg and wing bones. Press with the hand to open the chicken butterfly style. Push a satay stick or metal skewer through the chicken to hold it open.

Bring water to the boil in a wide pan together with the vinegar, wine, lime and syrup. Hold the chicken above the pan with one hand and use the other to scoop ladles full of the boiling liquid over the chicken to drench it thoroughly. Drain the chicken and leave to dry in the sun for 1 hour.

To prepare the **stuffing**, chop or blend the prawns to a paste, then combine with all other ingredients. When the chicken is dry, sprinkle a little additional cornflour on the inside to make the stuffing adhere, then spread an even layer of the stuffing over the inside of the chicken. Heat oil in a wok and deep fry the chicken over high heat until golden brown.

Cut into squares to serve, together with any commerical chilli sauce or Chilli Ginger Sauce (page 39).

Helpful hints: Do not remove the skewer when frying the chicken to ensure it holds its shape. If you prefer, de-boned and flattened chicken thighs can be substituted for the whole chicken.

AYAM PANGGANG

Barbecued Spicy Chicken

Barbecueing was a very common method among Malay cooks in the old days, when every *dapur* (kitchen) had a wood fire. These days, barbecued or *panggang* foods are more likely to be found at food stalls, where whole chickens are generally replaced by chicken wings or drumsticks. 🕐🕐

> 1 **whole young chicken, about 500 g (1 lb), or 2 chicken thighs with drumsticks attached**
> 2 **cloves garlic**
> 2.5 **cm (1 in) ginger**
> 1 **tablespoon lime juice, preferably from small round limes (*limau kesturi*)**
> ¹/₂ **teaspoon salt**

Spice Paste:

> 10 **bird's-eye chillies**
> 25 **red chillies**
> 15 **shallots**
> 10 **cloves garlic**
> 2 **tomatoes**
> 2 **tablespoons oil**
> 4 **tablespoon lime juice, preferably from small round limes (*limau kesturi*)**
> 1 **tablespoon sugar**
> **salt and pepper to taste**

Cut the chicken down the back. Remove the backbone and press the chicken out in butterfly shape. Alternatively, cut into quarters or large serving pieces. Pound or blend the garlic and ginger together, mix with lime juice and salt and rub into the chicken. Set aside.

To prepare the **spice paste**, put the chillies, shallots, garlic and tomatoes in a steamer and cook for 5 minutes. Slit the large red chillies and discard the seeds; remove the seeds from the tomatoes. Put steamed items in a blender and process coarsely.

Heat oil in a pan and stir fry the blended paste over low heat for about 5 minutes, until fragrant. Add lime juice, sugar, salt and pepper to taste.

Cook the chicken over charcoal for 5 minutes, turning half-way through. Rub chicken thoroughly on both sides with the cooked spice paste and leave for 5 minutes to allow the flavours to penetrate. Return chicken to the barbecue and cook until tender and golden brown on both sides.

Helpful hints: The spice paste can be prepared several hours in advance.

BRAISED CHICKEN IN POTATO MOULD

The ingredients and seasonings are typically Chinese and it is only the final treatment of this dish that shows an innovative approach, adding potatoes and baking the chicken. The chicken can be cooked well in advance and the dish finalised by preparing the potatoes and baking the assembled dish in the oven. 🕐 🕐

1 whole chicken, about 1.5 kg (3 lb), cut in pieces and de-boned
oil for deep frying
12 fresh *shiitake* mushrooms, quartered
10 button mushrooms, halved
6 cm (2½ in) ginger, sliced
750 g (1½ lb) large potatoes, peeled and thinly sliced lengthwise
1 tablespoon butter

Marinade:

2 tablespoons light soy sauce
1 tablespoon black soy sauce
2 tablespoons oyster sauce
1 egg, lightly beaten
salt and pepper to taste

Sauce:

1 tablespoon oil
5 cloves garlic, finely chopped
5 whole star anise
1 cinnamon stick, about 4 cm (1½ in) long
1 tablespoon five-spice powder
3 tablespoons oyster sauce

4 tablespoons Chinese wine
3 tablespoons light soy sauce
1 tablespoon black soy sauce
1 teaspoon sesame oil
2 teaspoons sugar
2 cups chicken stock
2 teaspoons cornflour, mixed with 2 tablespoons water

Combine the **marinade** ingredients, mix with the chicken and set aside to marinate for 10 minutes. Pat the chicken dry and deep fry in very hot oil until half cooked.

To prepare the **sauce**, heat 1 tablespoon oil in a saucepan and stir fry the garlic, star anise and cinnamon for 1 minute. Add the deep-fried chicken, both types of mushrooms and ginger. Stir fry for 3 minutes, then add remaining sauce ingredients except for cornflour. Simmer for about two minutes and season to taste, then add the blended cornflour. When the sauce thickens a little, remove from fire and set aside to cool.

Pan fry the thinly sliced potatoes with butter and oil until half cooked. Line an oven-proof bowl with the half cooked potatoes, making sure they overlap. Fill with the cooked chicken mixture and cover with remaining potatoes. Bake in a hot oven (200°C/ 400°F) for about 5–7 minutes. Unmould and serve hot.

AYAM LEMAK

Chicken in Coconut-milk Gravy

A wonderfully fragrant Malay dish which uses fresh roots and herbs rather than dried spices for its flavour. If you don't like your food fiery hot, reduce the amount of bird's-eye chillies. ⏱ ⏱

1 chicken, about 1.5 kg (3 lb), washed and cut into 12–14 pieces
10 shallots
8 cloves garlic
5 red chillies
2.5 cm (1 in) ginger
2.5 cm (1 in) fresh turmeric, or 1 teaspoon turmeric powder
2 tablespoons oil
5 fragrant lime leaves (*daun limau purut*)
2 lemon grass, bruised
2.5 cm (1 in) galangal, sliced
1 teaspoon coriander powder
2 cups water
3 cups coconut milk
salt and pepper to taste
5 green chillies, halved lengthwise
10 red or green bird's-eye chillies, left whole (optional)
fried shallots to garnish

Pat chicken dry and set aside. Chop then pound or blend the shallots, garlic, chillies, ginger and turmeric, adding a little of the oil if necessary to keep the blades turning. Heat the remaining oil and add the ground paste together with the lime leaves, lemon grass, galangal and coriander. Sauté for about 5 minutes until fragrant.

Add the chicken and sauté until it is well coated with the spices. Add water and simmer uncovered until the chicken is half cooked, then add the coconut milk. Season to taste with salt and pepper. When the chicken is almost cooked, add the green chillies and the whole bird's-eye chillies and continue cooking until tender. Serve sprinkled with fried shallots.

HAINANESE CHICKEN RICE

A Singapore classic which must be made with fresh chicken to achieve the perfect flavour and texture. This is always accompanied by rice cooked in the chicken stock, sliced cucumber, soup and three sauces, which each person mixes to taste. ⓔⓔ

1 fresh chicken weighing about 1.5 kg (3 lb)
1–1.5 litres (4–6 cups) chicken stock (page 40)
1 teaspoon light soy sauce
$\frac{1}{4}$ teaspoon sesame oil
sliced cucumber to garnish
finely sliced spring onion to garnish

Rice:

2 cups long-grain rice, well washed
chicken stock to cover

Sauces:

chilli ginger sauce (page 39)
5 cm (2 in) fresh ginger, blended with 1 table-
spoon water
2 tablespoons black soy sauce

Clean and dry the chicken. Bring a large pan of chicken stock to the boil and put in the chicken. Turn off the heat, cover the pan and let the chicken stand for 15 minutes. Remove chicken from the pan, plunge in iced water and drain. Bring the stock back to the boil, add the chicken and repeat the steeping process. Repeat the entire process another couple of times, so that the chicken has a total of 45 minutes steeping in the stock. By now, the chicken will be lightly cooked. Cut into serving pieces, sprinkle with the soy sauce and sesame oil and garnish with cucumber.

When the chicken is cooked, take enough of the stock to cook the **rice** following your favourite method.

Put each of the sauces in separate dishes. Serve the chicken at room temperature, accompanied by the hot rice, the sauces and the remaining stock, garnished with a little spring onion.

DUCK IN FRAGRANT SOY SAUCE

A Teochew favourite sometimes made with goose, this is a simple but very tasty way of simmering duck in soy sauce flavoured with "black" spices (cinnamon, star anise and cloves). The addition of fresh turmeric and lemon grass, which are Southeast Asian rather than Chinese seasonings, reflects the Singapore touch. ⊘⊘

    1 fresh duck, about 2 kg (4 lb)
    1 tablespoon five-spice powder
    7 cinnamon sticks about 8 cm (3 in) long
    15 star anise
    20 cloves
    10 shallots, lightly bruised
    10 cloves garlic, lightly bruised
    3 tablespoons *jin kok* (optional)
    4 cups light soy sauce
    3 tablespoons black soy sauce
    2 tablespoons sugar
    1 lemon grass, bruised
    5 cm (2 in) fresh turmeric, bruised, or
        2 teaspoons turmeric powder
    6 litres (24 cups) water

Clean the duck and rub the inside with the five-spice powder. Leave in the refrigerator overnight.

Rinse the duck inside and out with water and put in a large wide pan with all the seasonings and water. Bring to the boil and simmer gently, uncovered, until the duck is very tender. Serve with white rice.

Helpful hints: *Jin kok* is a dried Chinese root which should be available at a Chinese medicine shop or at some provision shops.

SATAY BABI

Pork Satay with Pineapple Sauce

Skewers of seasoned meat or chicken grilled over charcoal is one of Singapore's most popular Malay stall foods. This Nonya version is made with pork (not eaten by Muslims) and served with a sauce mixed with crushed pineapple. ☺☺

500 g (1 lb) pork fillet, cut in 48 cubes
1 lemon grass, sliced
8 shallots
2 teaspoons coriander powder
½ teaspoon turmeric powder
1 teaspoon salt
2 teaspoons brown sugar
4 tablespoons oil

Sauce:

8 dried chillies, soaked
8 shallots
1 clove garlic
4 candlenuts
1 lemon grass
2 tablespoons oil
1 cup coconut milk
1 tablespoon tamarind pulp soaked in 4 table-spoons water, squeezed and strained
1 teaspoon brown sugar
½ cup fried peanuts, coarsely ground, or ½ cup chunky peanut butter
salt to taste
¾ cup crushed pineapple

Put pork cubes in a bowl. Blend lemon grass and shallots, then mix with coriander, turmeric, salt, sugar and 1 tablespoon oil. Stir into pork and marinate for 2 hours. Soak satay skewers in cold water while pork is marinating to prevent them from burning during grilling.

Make **sauce** by blending chillies, shallots, garlic, candlenuts and lemon grass. Heat oil and fry blended ingredients for about 5 minutes, stirring occasionally. Add coconut milk and bring slowly to the boil, then put in tamarind juice, sugar, peanuts and salt. Simmer gently for a couple of minutes, then allow to cool before adding the crushed pineapple.

Thread the pork pieces onto bamboo skewers, brush with oil and cook over hot charcoal until done. Serve with the sauce and, if liked, chunks of cucumber and raw onion.

PORK RIBS FRIED IN PANDAN LEAVES

The elusive fragrance of pandan or screwpine leaves permeates a number of savoury rice, meat and chicken dishes of Malay or Nonya origin, while juice extracted from the leaf is often used in cakes and desserts. The use of pandan to wrap food (most often seasoned chicken) before deep frying has been borrowed relatively recently from Thailand. This Singapore adaptation uses pork ribs. ⊘ ⊘

1 kg (2 lb) pork ribs, cut in 4 cm (1½ in) pieces
8 cloves garlic
8 shallots
6 tablespoons honey
2 tablespoons red sweet sauce
1 tablespoons five-spice powder
3 tablespoons Lea & Perrins sauce
1 tablespoon HP sauce
2 tablespoons sour plum sauce
4 tablespoons oil
1 teaspoon sesame oil
24 pandan leaves
oil for deep frying

Choose meaty pork ribs and have them cut to the correct length. Pound or blend together the garlic and shallots, then mix with all other ingredients except pandan leaves and oil for deep frying. Leave to marinate for about 2 hours.

Wrap each of the pork ribs with pandan leaves, tying a simple knot and leaving about 15 cm (6 in) of the leaf protruding at one end. Fry in very hot oil for 3–5 minutes until cooked. Serve hot still in the pandan leaf, allowing each diner to unwrap his or her own portions.

Helpful hints: If you cannot obtain pandan leaves, use greaseproof baking paper cut in squares. Fold up the pork ribs envelope style and fasten with a staple before frying. Lea & Perrins sauce and HP sauce are both of English origin, but should be available in any gourmet shop—if not in supermarkets —in most countries.

BUNTUT ASAM PEDAS

Sour Hot Oxtail Stew

Oxtail has long been a popular Singapore dish, prepared as a vaguely English-style stew by Hainanese cooks. The rich flavour and faintly gelatinous texture of the oxtail is enhanced when it is cooked Malay/Indonesian style. 🕑🕑

1 whole oxtail, about 2 kg (4 lb), cut in 4 cm (1½ in) pieces
10 shallots
8 cloves garlic
25 red chillies, de-seeded
10 bird's eye chillies
2.5 cm (1 in) turmeric, or 1 teaspoon turmeric powder
3 tablespoons concentrated tomato paste
200 g (7 oz) tamarind pulp, soaked in 2 cups of water, squeezed and strained for juice
2 tablespoons sugar
5 fragrant lime leaves (*daun limau purut*)
2 lemon grass, bruised
4 cm (1½ in) galangal, sliced
3 litres (12 cups) water
salt and pepper to taste
fried shallots to garnish

Trim all fat off the oxtail and discard. Chop then pound or blend the shallots, garlic, chillies and turmeric, adding a little water if necessary to keep the blades turning. Combine the blended mixture with all other ingredients except water and mix well with the oxtail. Leave to marinate for 2 hours.

Bring the water to the boil in a large pot and add the marinated oxtail. Simmer uncovered over low heat until the oxtail is tender and the sauce thickens. Season to taste with salt and pepper. Simmer over slow fire until the oxtail is tender and the liquid is reduced by about half. Season to taste with salt and pepper and serve with white rice.

KAMBING KORMA
Indian Mutton Curry

A mixture of dried ground spices, whole spices and the usual trinity of shallots, garlic and ginger provide the basic flavourings for this rich mutton curry. The Singapore touch is evident in the use of candlenuts (not found in India) to enrich and thicken the gravy. ② ②

1 kg (2 lb) mutton or lamb, cubed
10 shallots
10 cloves garlic
5 cm (2 in) ginger
10 green chillies
3 tablespoons oil
1 large onion, sliced
6 cardamom pods, bruised
5 whole star anise
2 sticks cinnamon about 8 cm (3 in) long
4 tablespoons meat curry powder
20 curry leaves
3 potatoes, quartered
1 cup plain yoghurt
10 candlenuts, pounded or blended
2 slices *asam gelugor* or 1 tablespoon tamarind pulp, soaked in 4 tablespoons water, squeezed and strained for juice
4–6 green chillies, halved lengthwise
6 tomatoes, quartered
1 teaspoon salt

Put the mutton in a pan with 2 litres (8 cups) water. Chop then blend the shallots, garlic, ginger and 10 green chillies with a little water. Add to the mutton and bring to the boil. Simmer uncovered until the meat is just tender.

Heat oil and gently sauté the onion, cardamom, star anise, cinnamon, curry powder and curry leaves. When it smells fragrant, add to the meat together with the potatoes, yoghurt, salt, candlenuts and tamarind. Continue simmering until the meat is soft. Add the green chillies and tomatoes just before serving.

JACKFRUIT PUDDING & MANGO JELLIES

JACKFRUIT PUDDING

These cakes made with jackfruit (or other tropical fruit) make a pleasant snack or dessert. ②②

- **2 cups rice flour**
- **1 cup tapioca flour**
- **6 cups coconut milk**
- **6 pandan leaves or pandan essence to taste**
- **200 g diced jackfruit, mango or sliced banana**
- **30 sqares of banana leaf about 20 cm (8 in) square**
- **15 tablespoons thick coconut milk**
- **15 tablespoons palm sugar syrup (page 33)**
- **1 teaspoon salt**

Opposite:
Mango Jellies and Jackfruit Pudding (top left)

Combine the rice flour, tapioca flour, coconut milk, salt and pandan leaves and cook over low heat, stirring constantly, until very thick. Remove pandan leaves, cool slightly and add the jackfruit.

Place one banana leaf on top of the other and pile some of the cooked mixture in the centre. Pleat in both sides of the banana leaf. Pour in 1 tablespoon each of thick coconut milk and sugar syrup, then fasten with toothpicks to secure. Alternatively, roll in a cone but do not top with coconut milk and palm sugar, serving these separately.

Steam the bundles for 25 minutes. Allow to cool to room temperature or chill before serving.

MANGO JELLIES

Delicate and light, these can be garnished when serving to make an elegant dessert. **②②**

- **1 litre (4 cups) water**
- **200 g (7 oz) sugar**
- **30 g (1 oz) or 6 teaspoons gelatine, softened in warm water**
- **1 cup coconut milk**
- **$\frac{1}{2}$ cup evaporated milk**
- **2 eggs, beaten**
- **200 g (7 oz) mango pulp, puréed**
- **1 large mango, very finely diced**

Combine the water and sugar in a pan and stir over low heat until sugar is dissolved. Add soaked gelatine and continue heating until thoroughly dissolved. Remove from heat and add all ingredients except the diced mango. Mix until well blended then add the diced mango.

Pour into individual moulds and refrigerate until set. Garnish when serving with fresh fruit and a little mango purée.

ALMOND JELLY & RED BEAN DESSERT

ALMOND JELLY

A classic Chinese restaurant dish, this is very simple to make and can be prepared well in advance. What better choice to end a Chinese dinner! ⏱

> 1 litre (4 cups) water
> 3 teaspoons agar agar powder
> ½ cup sugar, or more to taste
> 1 teaspoon almond essence
> 1 tin longans or lychees
> ice cubes (optional)

Opposite:
*Red Bean Dessert
(left) and Almond
Jelly (top right)*

Put water in a saucepan and sprinkle with agar agar powder. Bring gently to the boil, stirring, then add the sugar and almond essence. Simmer for a minute then pour into a dish about 15 cm (6 in) square. Leave to set then refrigerate until required. Make sure the tin of fruit is also placed in the refrigerator.

Just before serving, put the chilled longans or lychees in a large bowl. Cut the almond jelly into squares and add to the fruit. Add a few ice cubes if liked and serve immediately.

RED BEAN DESSERT

This Chinese favourite, believed to be very nutritious, is more likely to be served as a between-meal snack or afternoon tea than as a dessert. ⏱

> 2 cups dried red azuki beans, soaked 1–2 hours
> 2½ litres (10 cups) water
> 250 g (8 oz) sugar
> 10 pandan leaves or pandan essence
> ½ cup coconut cream

Drain the soaked red beans and put into 2½ litres of water. Bring to the boil and simmer uncovered for 40 minutes. Add the sugar and pandan leaves and cook for a further 10 minutes. Put into individual bowls and serve while still warm. Accompany by coconut cream.

Helpful hints: Do not confuse the small red azuki beans with the much larger red kidney beans.

BUBUR CHA CHA & KUIH SERIMUKA
Coconut Milk with Yam & Rice with Coconut-milk Topping

BUBUR CHA CHA

If you're accustomed to thinking of yams and sweet potatoes as vegetables, this Nonya dessert may sound somewhat surprising. However, once these tubers are combined with coconut milk sweetened with palm sugar, they take on a whole new flavour. Some cooks also add a spoonful or two of coloured sago balls when the yam is half-cooked. ⏲ ⏲

200 g (7 oz) yam, peeled and diced
200 g (7 oz) sweet potato, peeled and diced
1 large sliced banana
2 cups water
¹⁄₂ cup chopped palm sugar
2 cups thick coconut milk
5 pandan leaves or pandan or vanilla essence

Opposite:
Kuih Serimuka (left) and Bubur Cha Cha (right).

Put the yam and sweet potato in a pan with the water and pandan leaves. Simmer until half cooked, then add the sugar and simmer until yam and sweet potato are tender. Add the banana together with coconut milk and heat slowly. If using essence rather than pandan leaves, add now.

Serve at room temperature in individual bowls.

KUIH SERIMUKA

Steamed glutinous rice is topped with a layer of rich coconut milk flavoured with pandan. ⏲ ⏲

500 g (1 lb) glutinous rice, well washed
1 cup coconut milk

Topping:
30 pandan leaves, blended and strained for juice
5 eggs, lightly beaten
1 cup coconut milk
1 cup sugar
60 g (2 oz) plain flour
¹⁄₂ teaspoon vanilla essence
green food colouring

Soak rice in cold water for 2 hours. Drain. Spread on a wet cloth inside a steamer and cook for 20 minutes. Put rice into a bowl and mix with the coconut milk. Return to the steamer and cook until tender. Transfer the rice into a dish, pressing down to make a layer about 2 cm (³⁄₄ in) thick.

Combine pandan juice with the remaining topping ingredients, mixing well. Poke holes in the layer of rice with a chopstick, then pour over the topping. Put inside a steamer and cook over gently boiling water for about 45 minutes. Leave aside to cool then store in the refrigerator.

Index

The following is an alphabetical listing of ingredients and food appearing in Part One and Part Two of this book. Local names are in italics. An alphabletical listing of recipes, in both English and local, can be found on page 131.

Alphabetical List of Recipes

This is a comprehensive listing, in both English and local languages of recipes appearing in Part Three of this book.